LEADERS
IN
TRANSITION

STEVE BROE

Copyright © 2012 Steve Broe
All rights reserved.

ISBN: 1468145495
ISBN-13: 9781468145496

Introduction for Leaders in Transition

"How did you become a leader after changing your career?"

I asked this question many times over the last few years. I met colleagues at Starbucks, and asked them while we both had warm caffeine. I created an online survey. I tweeted the question, and talked with interesting people who were willing to share their stories. I asked other friends, "Who do you know who became a leader after they changed their career?" I found many interesting answers.

I am a fan of leaders. I believe leaders contribute to making this a more satisfying world. Sure, there are bad leaders out there. However, the leaders I know are all trying to improve themselves while they change the world around them. Many people are just getting started as a leader, and they are trying out new skills tentatively, like a baby bird leaving its nest. I call these people, "emerging leaders."

I've talked to a sales executive, an elected official, and the executive director of a church. I talked to an NCIS agent. I've had coffee with several writers, and a healer. Their situations were quite different. Some of their stories were compelling.

I never got tired of asking people, "How did you become a leader?" I put some of the best answers in this book. I hope you enjoy what I've heard.

I have prepared this book with emerging leaders in mind. I know that many people have lost their jobs in the last few years, and some readers are ready to launch careers. To these people, I say, "Proceed with confidence and joy!" Consider becoming a leader in the process. This book may help you get there.

I also believe this book will help coaches, people considering a change, and anyone who counsels career- changers. In addition, anyone interested in becoming a leader ought to be interested in what I've heard from others.

We need more leaders. We need people who are willing to take a stand, work with others, and create a positive change for the community and world. In Leaders in Transition, the reader will discover five principles that have made a difference for emerging leaders. From my knowledge of published research on leadership, these principles are universal. These ideas will help anyone looking to practice the art of leading others.

One friend of mine claims that leadership is love. Anyone who cares enough to assume responsibilities to make the world better for others is serving in love. We offer love to the people we know, and the world beyond, by acting as a leader. Being a leader doesn't mean we have all the answers, or that one is always right. Leadership is about daring to do the right thing.

Scholar Warren Bennis has taught that leadership is an art form. It is a performance act that involves other people to permanently transform the world around us. Leaders may not have certainty, but with vision and values in mind, leaders know what is right. The art of leadership is finding the best way to get there.

To all of you changing careers or thinking about it, I hope you choose to be a leader. You may bring love and art into your world.

~ Dr. Steve Broe
October, 2011

Contents

Introduction for Leaders in Transition iii
Chapter 1 - A Positive Career Change 1
    The Risky World of Changing a Career
    and Transforming One's Life 6
    The Perils of Making a Career Transition 11
Chapter 2: What Are the Opportunities in
Making a Career Change? 17
    Greater Connection with Loved Ones 18
    Control Over One's Life 18
    Reclaiming Repressed Personality 19
    Fulfillment 20
    Important Words Used in This Book 21
    What Uou Will Find in This Book 23
Chapter 3: What Rules Can I Challenge? 25
Chapter 4: What is a Leader? 27
    What Does Being a Leader Mean to You? 29
    Your Future in Leadership 29
    Leaders are Uniquely Different from Each Other 31
    What Skills do You Need to be a Transformational Leader? .. 32
Chapter 5 - The Intentional Career Change 37
    How Does One Make an Intentional Career Transition? ... 38
    The Neutral Zone 47
    Emerging as a Leader 50
Chapter 6 : The Work of a Leader 51
    The Work of a Leader 51
    Five Practices of Leaders 51
    Careers by Choice 56
Chapter 7 Examine Leadership Myths 59
    The Leadership Well 63

Bust Those Myths – Draw on Your Own
    Source of Knowledge..65
Chapter 8 Connecting With Your People 67
  Power of Connections 69
  A Voice for Connection: John C. Maxwell 70
  Nathan's Story..71
  Lessons from Connecting 73
Chapter 9 Energy 79
  A Serial Entrepreneur Finds a Mission 82
  Find Your Purpose 83
  Share and Receive Energy from Other People...................84
  Get Energized by New Experiences.................................86
  Enjoy the Freedom of Making Your Own Choices 87
  Get Energized by Learning 88
  Energy Supports Career Breakthrough............................89
Chapter 10 Leaders Inspire Learning....................................91
  Kirk: A Journey from Hair Stylist to Science Educator 94
  The Work Must be Learned 96
  Have an Open Attitude Toward Learning
    the Lessons of Transition 97
  Learn About People 98
  Help Others Learn 99
  Be Adaptive 100
  Learning is a Performance Skill for Leaders 101
Chapter 11 – The Nature of Work 103
  A Patriot and a Cop 106
  Go Ahead, Work Hard...108
  Make Work a Priority..109
  Live Your Values..110
  Work with Politics and Obstacles.................................111
  Rise in the Hierarchy..112
  Work Can be a Pleasure 113
Chapter 12 Goals and Results...117
  From Corporate Citizen to Entrepreneur.......................119
  Know Your Long Term Goals.....................................121

Solve Problems 123
  Get Results for Clients 124
  Be Focused. Work Intentionally 125
  Have Financial Goals 126
  Put Your Goals in Writing 127
  Goals Lead You to Victory 128
Chapter 13 – Your Career Victory 133
  Victory Changes Everything 133
  Assessment 135
  Achieve Mental Clarity 137
  Begin with a Dream 142
Chapter 14 Questions to Lead the Leaders 143
  What Resources Have You Tapped Into? 146
  Would You be Open to New Changes in Your Life? 147
  Do You Know What Motivates the People in Your Life? ... 147
  How Are You Building Your Support System? 148
  What Qualities About You Span Both Careers? 149
  What Else is Important in the Transition Period? 150
  What Are the Thought Processes That Brought You Here? .. 150
Chapter 15 Some Thoughts on Changing Your Behavior ... 153
  Are You Really Ready to Make Changes,
     or Are You Flirting with the Concept? 154
  Do You Understand That Internal Change is
     Necessary to Changing Your Career? 154
  What do You Have to Change to Launch
     Your Career Move? 155
  Have You Crossed the Emotional Bridge?
     Have You Decided? 155
  Change is Tough. Are You Willing to be Disciplined? 156
  What Are Your Support Systems for Changing? 157
Chapter 16 Are You Becoming a Leader Yet? 159
Epilogue: The Storm and the Well 163
  Fears After the Storm 164
  In Transition, After the Storm 165
  The Storm Rocks Us; It is Not There for Comfort 167

The Authentic Leader in the Storm 168
Liberation After the Storm 169
The Liberated Spirit: Stay Open 171
The Resilient Spirit 172
A Look at Your Network After the Storm 172
Relationships Support Your Growth 175
Connecting with People 177
Finding Your Well 178
Sharing Your Well 179
The Light of the Vision 180
Closing Thought 181
References 183

Chapter 1 - A Positive Career Change

Do you know anyone who feels stuck in their work? People I've talked to tell me that jobs are meaningless. Their career doesn't challenge them professionally, and work doesn't offer a chance at growth. You've probably seen good people laid off; those people left behind wonder when they are going to get the pink slip. Workers who do keep their jobs often work long hours, covering for the people who no longer have their jobs. Many talented people are looking for a way out, a path to using satisfying lifetime work. I hear frustration and doubt in their voice, and I see fatigue and concern on their face.

You probably know someone who was successful at creating a new career. I was curious about how people make successful changes. I've held conversations with 33 people who have not only made a change to their career; they now call themselves a leader in what they do. I've been curious about what their secrets are. I talked to these career changers about what it took to make a change. Along with new kinds of work, I've had people tell me that they have become a leader in what they do when they changed jobs. I found hope and inspiration from their stories.

I've heard from these new leaders that *positive career change is possible*. They had dramatically different stories. Some worked in business, government, and education. Some of these career changers found a new job, opened a new business, or wrote a book. No one promised me that success was guaranteed. Everyone told me that the change was worth it.

> **DR. STEVE'S TIPS FOR LEADERS**
>
> Throughout this book, you'll find a pause in the reading with an important idea to guide you on your journey of career change and leadership.
>
> Leaders in Transition was built around the experiences of career changers. To create this book, I interviewed 33 people who became a leader after they changed their career. Their voices and ideas are found on these pages.
>
> As a career changer, you will face many choices. Your state of mind and your experience will influence the choices you know about. A leader tries to understand all the relevant choices that can help reach a successful goal.
>
> Think about the choices you have – and the choices that you haven't yet considered. How can you perceive more choices? Where can you get knowledge to help you reduce your risk?

Saul told me how he left the music business, and followed his passion for technology. Not only was he good with working with computers and software, he could show other people how to use their computers, too. Saul learned that he loved to help people solve problems with their technology. He went to work full-time helping people fix their software and technology problems at work and at home. After gaining skills and reputation in his new field, he now speaks at conferences and he trains other technology problem-solvers. Now he is a national leader in help-desk excellence. You'll meet Saul again in chapter ten as we consider the importance of learning.

Leaders are not solo artists. They work with other people, and change the way other people work. Some people are talented just working by themselves–an accountant, an engineer, or a researcher may not need to influence the way other people work. Leadership requires something more. Leaders engage people around them. I have found that working as a leader can be a highly satisfying way to make a big difference—a bigger difference than they could make by themselves. It can be fun and satisfying to inspire other people to get bigger results. The leaders I have talked to in preparing this book emerged as leaders in new career fields. They work with other people all the time, and they like it that way.

Do you find that the leader's work is meaningful? With any kind of work, leadership extends the circle of influence. An author changes the way other people write and think, and works as a thought leader. An office holder in state government (hopefully) makes the state a nicer place to live. A musician composes and performs a song that changes the way fans look at the world. Leaders of all kinds add meaning to the way we work, live, and relax. By the nature of their work, leaders cause those in their circles to have more meaningful lives.

Some people are very good at landing on their feet after a change. Many of us get seriously bruised along the way. In 1990, my transition was not a happy change, and it led to a full decade of regular changes. I wish I could say that my transition was something that I prepared for. Instead, I entered the turbulence of a stormy world of change without a good plan.

I was fired by a corporate vice president after working fourteen successful years in my family's business. I loved my work with Total Learning Centers. After building the business, expanding the revenues and developing great people, TLC was sold to a national chain of child care centers. I even helped sell it! The larger firm offered me a job as a regional manager–and fired me after just three months in my new position. Where was I going to go? I felt that my prospects for new employment were bleak.

Eventually, after nine months of searching, I was offered a position in another state as the vice president of a start-up chain of child care centers. I was promised an ownership position in the business. I moved my family, bought a new home, and I was disappointed again. The business promises were never fulfilled. Instead, the company entered bankruptcy within the year. The president of the company quickly turned into a hostile man, and I hated working for him. With an underemployed spouse, a young child, and a mortgage, I felt trapped by the cruelty of the turn of events. My trust in the company was drained after the year with the miserable company president (who was fired by the investors) and after working through the bankruptcy phase.

Just 18 months before, I had been a great manager, with an expanding business and work that lifted people's lives. I had creative projects, completed work that had meaning for me, and enjoyed an ethical clarity about how my work made the world a better place. My optimism crashed as I realized that I was completely unprepared for the life of transition.

I went from a great job to a bitter year of unemployment. I wanted to change people's lives, but I was stuck in a rut. My transition was painful. Eventually I found my equilibrium again, and came to enjoy my work under new circumstances.

I endured. My job eventually became happier and more secure. I developed support from new friends and colleagues; I managed to shift my work to focus on the areas that I enjoyed. I found satisfaction in work and by making new friends with other professional skills.

My career transition had been ugly and unplanned. Before my change, I thought my work was secure. I believed that even if my company were sold, my contribution before the sale would assure me of a great career with a new company. I discovered that I was naïve, which led me to several lean years of misery. I discovered that my new work was stable but not satisfying; I was worried about job loss or the terrible relationship with an ogre of a company president.

Through my career transition, I learned that I had a blind spot about my own future. I trusted that work would always be meaningful and secure for me. I had not prepared for my disruption, and went through a painful education accompanied by upheaval.

I had not paid attention to my inner world, nor declared what my future would look like.

This book is for people facing career transitions, who see themselves as leaders in the future. I have talked to thirty-three successful career changers, and asked about their path to victory. Change arrives on many levels. The prepared reader will move through change with less stress and greater joy. The person in career transition may work through several phases of change before he or she can emerge as a leader.

This book begins by exploring the social and psychological space of career transitions. Although every person's experience is unique, some emotional and intellectual processes are nearly universal for the transition experience. The process of career transition can be confusing. Some people emerge from their transition with a stronger network, new life skills, and a clear intention for a life purpose. With confusion as a starting place, leaders emerge. How do people make the most of their transitional period?

What does it mean to be a leader? Peter Drucker, in "The Leader of the Future" gave perhaps the best short answer,

"The only definition of a leader is someone who has followers."

Leaders are found in business, education, the military, and health settings. Any comprehensive discussion of leaders should be broad enough to include Winston Churchill, Mother Theresa, and even the Beatles. Leaders provide a vision, and change people's lives. In fact, the direction of change itself may be the essential work of a leader.

Leadership is not just about the capacity to give orders. Leaders frequently have power in the work that they do; power is often earned through a proven contribution to a purposeful enterprise. Power is not the defining quality of leadership, influence is. Effective leaders can encourage others to act independently and yet in alignment with their purpose, through the use of social influence.

This book includes the voice of leaders. Thirty-three leaders have been interviewed about their significant career change. Like you, I am interested in the life experiences that accompany a meaningful transition. Finding no modern answers to the question, "How do people make a career change and emerge as a leader?" I decided to explore the history and process of career change. In the later parts of this book, you will hear accounts from leaders about their transition experience. Learning from others is an insightful way to accelerate your own development as a leader after a career change.

THE RISKY WORLD OF CHANGING A CAREER AND TRANSFORMING ONE'S LIFE

More than just changing a job, a career transition marks a substantial shift in work. When a life story is reviewed, the transition is a complicated watershed moment. Life before and life after the transition are different, in more than superficial ways. A person's way of life shifts dramatically, and others are affected by the shake-up.

PERIOD OF DOUBT AND UNCERTAINTY

In a transition, the context of one's working arrangement shifts. Relationships between people are redefined–the old boss no longer has control over one's schedule, and friendships at work may end suddenly. Even the nature of "boss" and "working friendships" can be different. The old rules for social relationships may now be uncertain. Most importantly, one's certainty about the social role of the career now shifts dramatically. The person in transition does not hold a stable view of himself or herself.

During the nine months after I was fired, I experienced the turmoil of uncertainty. Much of my self-concept was connected to my work. I often questioned myself, wondering what my next job would be, and how I would make it creative and meaningful. After years of experiencing success in my work, I was suddenly adrift emotionally.

FINANCIAL INSECURITY

Until one has passed a few milestones, the person in transition often doubts the certainty of future flows of money, or stretches limited savings. During the period of transition, the person in change may be nervous about taking new risks, holding limited funds against future needs. The financial insecurity can serve to emotionally restrict any bold actions. During the period of transition, the number of choices may narrow to those permitted during a restrictive economy.

I worried about my financial standing after I left my first big job. With a young son, and a large house commitment, I knew that I had to recover my source of income quickly, or change my lifestyle radically. After securing a new job, I moved from a beautiful home in Newport Beach to the warm urban desert of central Arizona, which was hard for my wife, Carolyn.

EMOTIONAL TURBULENCE

The person in transition may vacillate between intentions of moving forward to a future new state, and a return to an older, known state. This back-and-forth experience is accompanied by feelings of hope and hopelessness. Emotions run up and down an intensity scale. Even as external circumstances shift toward different possible futures, the internal feeling of confidence may rocket skyward, or plummet rapidly, even during a period of a few hours.

All of us experience the emotional turmoil of change, and from lessons of emotional pain, we build our character, and prepare for future achievement. Leaders have fully emerged from the pain of internal conflict and emotional upheaval. The person who conquers his or her own distress and proceeds with courage is the person who can achieve greater goals in the future.

REDUCED TRUST

Our relationships with friends and coworkers can change during periods of career upheaval. Colleagues from work are reluctant to extend trust during periods of dramatic change, not wanting to place their allegiance or financial resources at risk. The person in transition can sense the emotional distance, and often withdraws trust from others.

One friend of mine operated a business successfully for a number of years, maintaining close relationships with many key employees. During a downturn, a bank forced a takeover of this business. Although still operating the company, the relationships with his employees changed. Business colleagues who had acted like family a few weeks before suddenly changed their relationships with my friend. He told me how surprised he was about how quickly and dramatically the sense of loyalty had turned with people he had worked with for years. Under these circumstances, trust was an early casualty of the transition.

CONFUSED SELF PERCEPTION

At times, the person in transition feels a pull to a future career position. At other moments, a sentimental longing for past security washes over the career changer. Even though the person in career transition hopes to move on to the next phase of his or her life, the idyllic memory of secure moments pushes the worker in transition back to a wistful longing for the past. While feeling the push and pull of career outcomes, the person in career transition continues to reevaluate the value of the past and future. Self-perception of one's capabilities can be confusing during this period.

During my year of unemployment, I wondered, "What would I be happy doing? How can I move forward? How can I get back what I lost?" Some of the hardest work I did was to continue working on my future work while feeling defeated inside. I wondered who I was underneath all the tides of feeling that moved through me regularly.

STRAINED RELATIONSHIPS

While the person in transition needs supportive time with loved ones, family and friends may not understand the internal tempest felt by the person in career transition. Some give advice, while the person in career transition may simply need to know that others will support the person emotionally during periods of upheaval.

My wife's cousin was divorced during a job change. His relationship with his wife may not have been perfect–whose marriage is?–and the stress of his career transition led to a painful breakup. In addition to challenges to his confidence from work, this man now endured a divorce and a forced distance from his children. Marital and family strains can certainly slow the process of career transition, as the person in career transition has diminished support from those closest.

Not all career changes are voluntary. Some people are fired, as I was. Others feel they must leave their work rapidly. One colleague of mine told me that she faced sexual harassment in her government job. She discovered that rude comments were made about her routinely–yet her knowledge for the work and section was top quality. The atmosphere became repellant to her, and she could not do her best work. She chose to start a new career at that time; fortunately, she had been preparing for a change. Because she had prepared herself for a new career interest, she took this occasion as the time to cut ties with being employed, and pursue her dream work full time. She made a voluntary separation but she had felt compelled to leave the agency. Even those of us who voluntarily separate may feel that the conditions do not allow a completely free choice.

Career transitions are watershed experiences for most of us. Life seems to work by different rules, depending on from what side of the transition one is gazing at one's career. During the transition, work is not the only change. The person in career transition also changes. Different aspects of life come to be more important. As well as changing how one views oneself, the person in career transition may recognize and celebrate new life milestones.

In transition, career transitioners sometime shift their life values. Those values inform the emerging leader how to plan, decide, and act.

Why do values change? We are all maturing, and as we face life challenges, we may come to value the creation of a personal legacy. The younger person often seeks immediate career rewards, while the person in midcareer longs to find new work that satisfies high order needs. The younger person may want promotion and benefits, while the person in midcareer may look for involvement in a nonprofit organization known for its good works. The midcareer transitioner often wants to contribute to important work, and to see his or her influence on something good.

The shift in values is not simply an act of replacing old values for new ones. The change in values is often a reordering of priorities. The new set of values may be familiar, but have a new sense of importance. Career transition often arises because some values, previously held but not satisfied, now demand greater fulfillment.

As the person in transition embraces the new values and their priorities, the world may seem different. The work of transition can cause one to shift perspective. When values assume new priorities, the reasons for working and taking actions may feel new, too. Although familiar values have been present before, the person in career transition has now reconfigured the relative order of the importance of those values. The values have a different emotional and motivational pull on the worker. Career change often shifts one's values.

The person in transition may feel a draw to long-unfulfilled dreams. When values shift in importance, the person in career transition recalls long-held yearnings. Perhaps the person in career transition made quiet personal promises, and never expressed those commitments to others. Dreams capture part of our energy, and until fulfilled (or released), dreams continue to pull on one's conscience. As the person in transition examines his or her values, the dream may return. He or she may recall, "I always wanted to be a doctor, and save lives." The return of a long-held dream may influence decisions and shape actions for the person in career transition.

One of my colleagues volunteers his free hours at the emergency room of a major hospital. We have never spoken about his life dreams; he may have an unfilled dream of becoming a doctor. He is a grandfather, divorced in the last decade, and has no interest in remarrying. My friend has great relations with his children and grandchildren, and holds a job that accords him respect and some independence. I know that he finds fulfillment with his time at the hospital. I wonder if he once wanted to be a doctor.

During time of transition, it is fitting that people seek to fulfill their early dreams. The person in career transition may feel satisfied in a manner that appeals to one's fundamental character. Dreams continue to have an appeal in life as our secure and stable past is rocked. During transition, it is right that one looks to complete long-held wishes. Perhaps if the dream feels distant from life, the person in career transition will take a major step towards the dream. That step which affirms the life dream may come to have growing importance.

Transitions arrive with a pair of emotional pulls: hope and anxiety. Hope draws us forward, as we match our dreams to the chance that circumstances can deliver our dreams in living form. Anxiety is the half-sister to hope, as career transition offers no certain future. The person in transition often wonders when the economy will break in his or her favor. During my lengthy unemployment period, I learned to manage my emotional state. Anxieties could pull me down; however, I needed to present an optimistic front to best welcome new opportunities.

THE PERILS OF MAKING A CAREER TRANSITION

Do you play golf? Along with the thrill of hitting a power stroke, you have surely felt the anguish of the water trap and the sand pit. A career transition has its great opportunities, yet the hazards are real.

As I moved through my career transition, I believed that better times were ahead. I became philosophical, choosing to learn and grow through moments of pain. I recall holding pithy thoughts like, "This too shall pass," and "Whenever one door closes, another one opens."

I understood also that complacency is dangerous. Without a plan of definite action, the belief in a balanced and fair universe can lead one to miss opportunity or change in the necessary direction. The career transitioner may embrace positive, life-affirming qualities, but also needs to work diligently to meet the future. When new skills are mastered, action toward goals will accelerate learning, providing the breaks needed to score a win.

LOSS OF INCOME

Optimistic plans and a clear vision help people move forward; however, the person in career transition also faces the loss of income while he or she sets up a new career. The income loss, or the threat of lost income, may force the person in career transition to avoid otherwise reasonable risks. Calculated risks are common on the journey of career transition. A danger for the person in career transition is becoming too cautious. Some risk-taking is necessary!

Worthwhile change builds on new behaviors, which the person in career transition explores intentionally. The person in transition must balance the threat of limited income with the need to invest in a new direction. Some of the change behaviors may be new for the person in career transition. The fear of financial ruin can put a chill on bold actions in a forward direction, at exactly the time a person must change the way he or she works.

UNFULFILLED DREAMS

This danger may be easily dismissed. Is a man or woman's dream important? I believe that the career changer should understand and honor dreams, and respect dreams for their driving power and value in our lives. A person without a dream may fail to reach greatness.

When a person attempts to achieve a dream and fails to reach the goal, the career transitioner may doubt or even reject the dream. **Dreams are a long-term project.** Most of us continue to work on our dreams, moving closer in steps. Sometimes the change of career transition is confusing, and the progress toward a dream may be hard to estimate.

How do we make dreams attainable? Some perspective in both time and position may help the person assess real gains. The person in career transition may need to seek guidance from a mentor, coach, or a business teacher to reflect on the progress toward career dreams.

Sometimes we shift our work and position, realigning our values as we grow, and our dreams still feel like they are unattainable. Growth can arrive without giving the person in career transition a clear advantage toward dream attainment. Even if a person makes an important work shift, and the dream seems no closer, one may be preparing to advance toward a life dream below the surface of actions and behaviors.

Take heart, if your dream has not yet surfaced into your waking life. Nurture the possibility that your life will produce the results you seek. Do not reject your dreams during a hard phase of career transition. **Stay connected with your important visions of life.**

DAMAGE TO SELF-ESTEEM

The person in career transition moves through an area uncharted, and the route may be risky to one's self-esteem. Old friends may dismiss the transitioner with prejudice and judgments, family members may tell him or her to look for a paid job (any job), and prospective clients can delay endlessly, avoiding a contract decision. After working weeks with continuous rejection, the person in transition will need self-esteem recovery.

While the person in career transition chooses change in the patterns of work, self-esteem may feel fragile and uncertain.

Rejection and doubts are certain to batter anyone's feeling of self-worth. When one follows a new dream, the old assumptions that make one secure are fundamentally challenged. The workplace batters the self-esteem of a person who breaks his or her old career patterns. Rough moments will appear during any transition. A strategy for overcoming self-esteem damage is to seek restoration and resilience.

Some people have resilience in abundance. When they fall down, they always get back up–quickly. I feel that my equilibrium returns slowly. My guess is that some people have ample emotional reserves, and others return to their center on a slower schedule. Do you find that your self-esteem is protected in times of change?

What increases your resiliency? For me, I believe that plenty of sleep and regular meditation have restorative qualities. I work out regularly; I am diabetic, and I've chosen to work out every day with either a cardiovascular or strength resistance training. These actions help reduce my recovery time after a psychic bruising. My self-esteem still bruises from ordinary living; I can lessen my downtime by paying attention to my internal energy.

A second factor I developed helps me moderate my self-esteem damage. I manage my emotions, especially when excessive change challenges my feelings of wholeness. Emotion management allows me to note my internal reactions to rough moments. If I am ignored when I expect praise, I remind myself to get on with what is important. Life is not about *me*. When I hear something hurtful, I tell myself that I am bigger than these momentary slams. Emotion management gives me perspective; I need to act, and take control of my emotional life. While I still hurt from the insults felt in life, I look beyond the moment. I decide to act despite the pain.

LESSONS FOR LEADERS

Career change is a path that involves risks and perils. Stepping into a new type and kind of work leaves one feeling vulnerable. Reduce your risk by reviewing your choices, choosing wisely, and work with supportive people who have made a similar journey before you.

Chapter 2 - What Are the Opportunities in Making a Career Change?

Train yourself to ask hard questions. "Do you see yourself doing this job for the next ten to twenty years?" When some people shift their perspective from the immediate (now until the next vacation) to the long term, people discover compelling reasons to make new plans. The opportunities for change may present hazards as well as fulfillment.

The benefits for making a career change are uniquely personal. The life experience of a career changer influences every opportunity. Here are some of the reasons that push people to start their transition.

> **DR. STEVE'S TIPS FOR LEADERS**
>
> Your career change should be about more than money. If you want to be a leader, your life will help other people. Leaders have the advantage of finding fulfillment in their work. They make the world a better place. The journey of a leader through career change often begins with personal needs and desires. As the journey matures, the emerging leader comes to see that other people are affected by his or her choices. Find the fulfillment in this work. Become passionate about the change you are creating for yourself and sharing with others.

GREATER CONNECTION WITH LOVED ONES

Career changers depend on other people to reach their goals. To change a career, people need a network of caring support. The career changer's friends and family may need to provide income, answer doubts at two o'clock in the morning, take over more chores at home, or serve as unpaid employees in a new business. Over and over, I have heard successful people tell me about the great help received from the people who stood with them while they took on new challenges. During a career change, the person in transition may deepen love for his or her spouse. The career changer often has to establish new working habits and schedules. The people at home make this experience positive and joyful, or add misery, depending on the attitude. After a painful job, or a destructive career phase, support from loved ones will deepen already strong relationships. Gratitude expands family ties.

CONTROL OVER ONE'S LIFE

When we work, we trade our free time for a reliable paycheck. Businesses need to control the use of working time. Bosses do not get much praise in our culture; they are paid to control us. A constant presence of management control may suppress the yearning for freedom and creative expression.

The career transition may be a bid to recover control. When starting a new career, a person can adopt new rules for work, new standards of discipline, and choose new communication tones with managers and customers. During the negotiation phase of a new job, one may stress control over working conditions. The mature career changer may also evaluate potential new bosses or major clients, and anticipate how controlling they will act over the new career. With knowledge and inner inspiration, the person in career transition stands a good chance of claiming more control over his or her life after an important change.

The career changer may claim control in at least three areas. First, one can now control one's own time, and schedule daily events as needed. The control of time allows one to make strategic choices in life. With new uses and priorities for time, the career changer has an opportunity for greater productivity and creative expression.

Second, the career changer may be able to take more risks. If he or she needs to commit time, money, or other work resources to an idea, life change may allow a certain project to advance. Relaxation from earlier restraints allows the career changer to become active in new ways. In a new career, the career-changer should take more risks that help one reach important goals.

Third, the career changer now has greater freedom to make choices. Held accountable to the confines of a new career choice and a personal set of priorities, the freedom to choose allows the career changer more leeway to act. Some people waste time in the effort to expand their freedom in a controlling workplace. A better strategy might be to find a less restrictive place to work, one that allows more energy for productive activities.

RECLAIMING REPRESSED PERSONALITY

The career changer may receive a great gift after leaving a job. What has been repressed, returns. We are all complex individuals; the employer may only need to hire part of our potential. In some jobs, the worker may come to understand that he is not to think, feel, or evaluate what happens, "just follow my instructions, repeat after me!" When this happens, the worker likely hides parts of his or her personality. Freud and his followers have called this act "repression." Repression always robs of us our energy and enthusiasm. The career changer gets some of this energy and enthusiasm back, realizing what they have hidden for years before.

One of my colleagues has toiled for years at a telephone call center. Thomas is a skilled musician with an MBA. Every time I have talked to him about his career, he has told me how much he hated his work. Thomas was not allowed to use his artistic side at his job. His employer only valued part of his talents; Thomas did not feel fulfilled! He rightfully felt the job only valued part of him.

He did not even get to use much of his talent as a careful decision-maker suggested by his MBA training. Is it any surprise that he was frustrated to work there?

Do you have talents fitting for your work that are not used? Perhaps after a career change, you will examine your skills and discover that some of your potential is lying dormant. One banker, working through a goals exercise, told me that he wanted to leave finance, and run a fishing business in Key West, Florida! Closing the door to a current career may open the door to your talents—talents that are waiting to delight you with your own brilliance.

Be open to possibilities. Some new skills may not have much career value, especially when viewed from an old perspective. I started practicing my clarinet in the 90s after letting it collect dust for three decades, and then I put it aside while I worked on my doctorate. Returning to music, I find the clarinet gives me a channel to think in fresh ways. Even when I am exhausted from a full day's labor, my time with my instrument does not seem a drain on my mind; I am invigorated. I get a bonus, too. After practicing, I notice the etudes I have been working on suggest a fresh pattern of thinking and acting. Music inspires me to perform in fresh ways.

FULFILLMENT

As people get older, their interest in meaningful work increases. The midcareer change may arise from a need to be fulfilled. Early career choices may have been selected because they provided a good income, status, and an opportunity to advance a career. Maslow's hierarchy of needs predicts that people will first fill safety needs (food, water, physical protection). As the worker satisfies lower level needs, a person will turn to affiliation and esteem needs, such as one might achieve in the first decades of one's career. Maslovian theory predicts that one will not turn to a higher-level need until the lower level need has been satisfied.

The yearning for meaningful work resembles self-actualization needs. A person who has enjoyed many of the milestones of a good career will be satisfied with safety, affiliation, and esteem needs. A person who has worked such a path for twenty years might ask, "What's next for me?" A self-actualizing person will look for a higher purpose, and seek to experience creative contributions that involve previously-hidden talents. In the pursuit of self-actualization, a person might plan for a change that directs one to contribute to a better world.

Career changers often work hard to seek fulfillment. Their choice to live a deeper life, one that works in accord with values and inspiring acts, may be only faintly understood when confronting some of the doubt of the transition.

IMPORTANT WORDS USED IN THIS BOOK

Before we go much further, let us make sure that we are talking about the same issues. I wrote this book to help people proceed through a career change, and become a leader in the experience. I take a broad view of the terms "career change" and "leadership" in this work, discovering with commentary about the transition as reported by my respondent group.

CAREER CHANGE

A career change is different from a promotion, a sideways transfer, or new job responsibilities. The person in a career change can expect to perform new duties, possibly in a new industry. A career change may mean a move from work as an employee to a self-employed individual, perhaps changing into a business owner or becoming an investor.

The person in a career change may straddle one career while launching a separate business. Unlike a job change marked by the definite beginning and ending of a job, the career change may be gradual, taking months and years to reach culmination. Many Americans launch a multilevel marketing business while continuing to depend on a regular paycheck. One independent professional keeps a day job working in information technology while developing a storefront business with regular hours and a webpage. A conductor of military and community orchestras also works as a real estate professional.

The career change usually will provide greater freedom of choice, greater passion, and greater control of time. When the career change is a choice not arising from a layoff, most people will seek expanded freedom. People select new careers because they are positive about their opportunity to build a better life.

LEADERSHIP

We can find leaders everywhere–and not just in the corporate headquarters. A leader is not a person approved to bark out orders. A leader influences others without the need for power. Career changers become leaders when their life experience and character growth makes the person a legitimate source for to guide others. As Billie Holliday told us in song, singing the blues is an earned right. Leadership works in the same way.

Managers and leaders do similar work, but they are not the same. Workers often confuse the two terms. Leaders define a method of working, changing it when necessary, and share their forward-looking vision of change. A manager often works to preserve the ways that work flows, seeking to make it efficient. Leaders can be managers, and conversely, managers can be leaders. I like Warren Bennis's (*On Becoming a Leader,* 1994) observation that "Managers do things right; leaders do the right things." Another way of expressing this observation is that managers seek to answer questions, while leaders seek to ask them.

A manager may grow into a leader. Many students of leadership proclaim, "Leaders are not born, they are grown." I share this opinion–the art and science of leadership follows life learning, often painful, earned from the challenge of hiring, firing, and failures. Vaill (1996) describes leaderly learning as an event that happens at the "process frontier," where change appears rapidly and with some danger to the working person. The challenge of learning at the point of pain and peril forces many managers to grow into leaders.

WHAT YOU WILL FIND IN THIS BOOK

I have prepared *Leaders in Transition* to notice and encourage leadership among people who considering a career change. I began this book in the middle of 2009, in an era when unemployment approached 10 percent of the workforce. In recent years, the unemployment rate was much lower. Because of uncertainty, economic upheaval, government takeovers and bankruptcies, many skilled people have considered a major career change. Some of these people will enter a new field. Some of the new generation of career changers will start a business, buy a franchise, start a partnership with a trusted colleague, or follow a dream.

Not everyone seeks to become a leader. Some who seek a career change may discover that they have done a good job in their transition, and whether they have sought a constituency, they now have followers. Others will move into a new position that requires them to lead other people. Some people seek positions of leadership; others find that they must become a leader to succeed. For any person involved in making a career change, this book may help the person in career transition succeed and become a leader of others. The leadership journey often involves answering the question, "Why do I do this?" and answering in a meaningful way.

The material from this book includes the voice of career changing leaders. I have sought people who have taken risks, started their business, or found a new career. I have interviewed dozens of these career-changing leaders to prepare this book. I have listened for decisive moments, milestones that reflect a real achievement, and insights from people who have worked at the process frontier.

You will find the real voice of leaders in this book, guidance for you as you meet your important challenges. These leaders speak to you across the pages. These people have been through the crucible, taken risks, and learned the hard way. I have located powerful ideas that have helped career changers advance toward their life dreams. Review these ideas. Look for guidance that can help you act.

> **LESSONS FOR LEADERS**
>
> *Be a good listener — to the right people. Informed people can offer support and wisdom. If you are creating a new path into your future, people who understand what it means to trail-blaze a new path can encourage you to take the right steps.*
>
> *Find the right people to listen to. Some friends in your life have never faced a career change as profound as the one you are choosing. These people do not have the voice of experience, and they will probably tell you to stick with security, and avoid transformational change. Make sure your guides understand the depth of the journey you are making.*

Chapter 3 - What Rules Can I Challenge?

Thinking about a career change? Don't make it harder by imposing special rules on the process. Are you restricting yourself with these rules? Think again.

> **DR. STEVE'S TIPS FOR LEADERS**
> Don't make life harder by adding unnecessary rules.

You need to quit your job first. Changing careers probably involves quitting your job at some point. But why eliminate your safety net early? Quitting your job does give you extra time at your disposal, but it may leave you feeling uncertain. Don't jump into the neutral zone before you're ready. Take a calculated risk in favor of your success, on your terms. Quit your job when the time is right.

You must be able to support yourself for six months to two years before you change careers. Financial security is excellent if you can get it. You won't know in advance how much security you'll need. Do take financial considerations into account. Perhaps you have an excellent support system. Some of the career changers started making money immediately after leaving their secure job. There are few guarantees, but the effective career changers I've talked to all took a calculated gamble on their own capability to make money.

You must have a business plan or a career plan before you change careers. Not a bad idea. Planning is a good practice, and a written plan has a substantial edge over mere thoughts. Planning prepares the mind, and increases the chances of reaching one's objectives. However, the career changer may learn a lot in the process of transition. Some people need to take action, and aiming comes afterward. Taking action may send one into a minefield–and being in a risky spot is an excellent reason to learn! The career changer will be helped with a plan, but the need to take immediate action could be more important than the value of a plan at the start.

You must have lots of self-confidence. Not true. Successful people often earn their self-confidence as they move toward their dream. Some of the career-changers I interviewed started with plenty of doubts, and found support with the people closest to them. Others launched their career change with ample confidence, and never doubted that they could make it. Don't wait for self-confidence to move you forward. Some people eventually earn their self-confidence as they see their goal line getting closer. Self-confidence may need to be built up as you take action. Look instead to the quality of your dream.

You must be over 25 and under 45. Older people have earned more experience. Younger people often have more energy. Both experience and energy are success factors. Don't discount your talent. Let your dream drive you forward.

> **LESSONS FOR LEADERS**
> *Go beyond the rules. Who told you to live with those rules anyway? Create your own reality.*

Chapter 4 - What is a Leader?

"Are you nuts?" My brother-in-law thought I was crazy when I announced that I was studying leadership. "When I think of leaders, I see some angry guy barking out orders to meek workers." If your idea of a leader is close to my brother-in-law's image, pay attention for a moment. That person who barks out commands is using the power of his position to force people to act. If he leaves the room, how long are the workers going to follow his command? If I were among the meek, I would take the first opportunity to rebel. I don't like people who use power over me!

A good leader has the ability to influence others, and followers may never feel that the leader uses power to make them work. Have you ever had a bad boss? Someone who wields power over you does not influence your feelings and motivation. A boss who uses power may not be a good leader unless he or she also knows how to ask you to cooperate. A good leader enlists the heart and mind of followers, and may even create new leaders. Making workers labor for eight hours with a spear at the back is an example of raw power, not good leadership.

Leaders challenge and engage people. The influence of a leader may be high or low depending on the mental attitude and readiness of the follower. Just as there are great musicians and lesser musicians, great doctors and average doctors, great poets and mundane poets, so is leadership a matter of degree. Not everyone will follow a leader, but the leader is still doing the work of leadership.

> **DR. STEVE'S TIPS FOR LEADERS**
>
> You have a future as a leader, if you want it.
>
> Leaders are made. If you want to live a life bringing positive change to the people you know, become a leader. Make the decision to step out, and keep learning.
>
> Most leaders I know are influential, emotionally connected to others, have a positive view of the future, challenge others to grow, and relate to others with integrity.
>
> If you don't describe yourself in these ways now, start. This is the curriculum for the rest of your life.

Are you a leader? You do not have to be a boss, command power, or be the focus of a *Time* magazine essay. As a leader, people may have talked about your ideas, and taken action. Perhaps you are the person in your organization about whom everyone says, "What does Joe think about this?" One friend of mine started a sole provider / professional business without any employees. She told me that she is a leader because she is well-known, others have followed her example, and other professionals defer to her as a person of knowledge and experience.

Leaders make a difference, they change the status quo, and they do not need employees to apply their leverage to action and results in the rest of the world. Victor Hugo wrote, "There is nothing more powerful than an idea whose time has come." Leaders provide us with powerful ideas. Leaders take us to the future.

WHAT DOES BEING A LEADER MEAN TO YOU?

For some people, being a leader means "being in command of others." It is true that leaders often end up having the power of command. However, good leadership probably starts with internal qualities. A person who is inspirational, understands others, shares powerful ideas, and invests other people with the ability to move forward–this person may be promoted into a position of power based on his or her people skills. The emerging leader may become successful in business, and hire others to help achieve goals. Other leaders may influence others through writing, speaking, or music–as did the Beatles.

I like Drucker's definition of leadership: a leader has followers. The definition is broad enough to include a broad range work and activities. Leadership shows up in many forms, with many different kinds of followers. A follower could be a banker, a yoga practitioner, a girl scout, or a political savant.

Are you interested in changing people's lives, or having power over them?

If you are working on a transition, you are changing your life in an important way. You may not be working for another person, or perhaps you have moved into nonprofit management. You may be selling through network marketing, or helping other people succeed through advertising. You can still be a leader.

YOUR FUTURE IN LEADERSHIP

Some qualities of leadership that may describe you in your new role:

INFLUENTIAL

Others listen to your ideas. You have the ability to shift people's opinions, or at least to encourage others to consider new possibilities. Your colleagues hold a positive regard for your position, and copy your actions.

EMOTIONALLY CONNECTED

You understand other's feelings. You understand your own emotional climate, and act authentically with what you feel. Somehow, you are able to transfer your emotional experience. The connection has a positive feeling for most of the people you know.

A POSITIVE VIEW OF THE FUTURE

You have a view of a better world, and you understand how to take people there. You talk and write about this positive view, and others begin to share your ideas. Your business or professional life serves this positive view. Your positive view is deep, based on life-changing reflection and work. You help other people feel that their work is important, too.

CHALLENGE OTHER PEOPLE TO GROW

When you work with other people, they add new skills, and try new behaviors. You help people expand their potential to do greater work. Some of your followers start to act as leaders themselves. You create new leaders who share some of your views!

AMBITION, COMPETENCE, AND INTEGRITY

According to Bennis and Goldsmith (2003), leaders have three essential qualities. We can expect that people who display ambition, competence, and integrity are leaders. **Ambition** is a proxy for action. A person with ambition has the drive to finish big projects. The quality of **competence** tells us the person is good at his or her craft. Competence sounds like faint praise, not much of a recommendation. Competence tells us the person expresses multiple talents. The leader may not be superior in all areas; however, we would expect the leader to perform at a moderate level, or better, in most work activities.

A leader should also have **integrity**. The leader shows that he or she is a reliable ally at work by holding some values as sacred. When a person authentically reflects these values by action and word, others will respect the leader as a person of principle. Integrity proves that the leader is trustworthy.

LEADERS ARE UNIQUELY DIFFERENT FROM EACH OTHER

Leaders are as different from each other as the different places people work. The general manager of a baseball team will be different from the artistic director of an opera. The senior partner at a legal firm will be different from the leader at a labor union.

Experiences change all of us. When you work through a career change, your focus of work will change, you may need to build new skills, and your self-perception will shift as you move into your new work. Personal change is unavoidable. Perhaps the way you work with other people will change as well. Expect to grow.

Many of us remember a great teacher or mentor who influenced the way we work. Although "bad boss" stories are legion, I had a great boss in my 20s who challenged me to do great work. Perhaps you had a great boss too, and you copy that person. Role models provide a vivid demonstration of work with an expert. As you grow, you may look to role models and ask, "What would my mentor do?" Although not a perfect guidance, we can find inspiration from the examples that have shaped us.

Consider becoming an intentional leader. Leaders change the lives of people. If your vision is transformational, you can change the world around you and encourage others to follow your example.

Think about your role as a leader. What does the career need? What do your colleagues need? Decide in advance how you will influence other people. You may want to clarify the core values that guide your decisions. Stephen Covey's (1992) *Principle-Centered Leadership* is an excellent guidebook for the reflective journey of a leader. Realize that if your transition is successful, you will be a role model for others. The beginning of your journey may set the tone for the transformation you set up for your followers. Be a conscious leader; include the thought of your role as a leader and mentor to others as you visualize your journey of creating a new career.

WHAT SKILLS DO YOU NEED TO BE A TRANSFORMATIONAL LEADER?

Professional writing on leadership suggests there are many different skills displayed by leaders. Big lists of leadership skills have been published in many books and professional journals. I am doubtful that studying lists of leadership traits builds leadership. People who believe in their purpose act like leaders. The skills you need will affect the work you do. Your relationship with your followers will depend on how much knowledge they have about their work.

I recommend that you become a transformational leader. A transformational leader is one that successfully changes the nature of the work, the organization, the community, or the world. The transformational leader aligns views of different people, in order that they may serve a greater purpose. Bass (1999) identified three qualities found in transformational leaders. These may be excellent skills to develop if you are entering transition.

INSPIRATION

A leader often can inspire others. Inspiration connects the heart and mind toward a big purpose. Followers find inspiration to start working after sharing ideas with a leader who lifts others through ideas. Followers and leaders who share an inspirational idea often feel connected to an important purpose.

Leaders in transition can communicate inspirational ideas. A person who has identified core values and has worked to further those values in the world may make decisions easily. Inspirational leaders know why their ideas are important. A leader can inspire others by showing how ordinary work serves a larger purpose.

An oft-repeated story describes how a traveler in a medieval age talks to several laborers on a construction site. The traveler asks, "What are you working on?" One laborer answers that he is building a wall. A second laborer, performing the same task, answers that he is building a church. A third answers that he is building a cathedral, "to provide a lasting place of worship and to glorify God." The third laborer found inspiration about his work and its lasting impact, and would likely have a greater investment in the quality of the work performed.

INTELLECTUAL STIMULATION

Transformational leaders do not just deliver orders; they provide details about the work, providing a look into "the guts of the machine." Intellectual stimulation delights the mind, and creates further thinking about all efforts. An intellectually stimulating leader might achieve this end by asking questions, challenging others to think and to discuss work. Followers who have worked in an environment of intellectual stimulation have greater understanding of the details, plans, and nuances of the strategy.

In schools, instructional leaders find ways to expand knowledge of the curriculum with teachers. The work of an instructional leader is to deepen how one understands and acts upon an educational program, helping teachers share best practices and strategies with challenging students. An instructional leader must provide intellectual stimulation to the other teachers, leaving a substantial understanding of the methods of the curriculum.

Intellectual stimulation is not just a good idea; knowledge workers and their managers need to receive intellectual stimulation to do their best work. Technology leads to changes, and many workers are affected when the technology is replaced rapidly. The leader who provides intellectual stimulation may show others how to become more skillful. Provide intellectual stimulation through discussion, training, and personal attention. Help workers talk to master practitioners. Workers can also learn through help files, software tools, and printed documents. The transformational leader ensures that followers have a quantity and diverse range of written support materials to challenge different kinds of learners.

TREAT EVERYONE AS INDIVIDUALS.

The transformational leader cares about people, and shows it in unique ways. Every person has a unique constellation of interests, dreams, and motivational causes. The effective leader tries to understand followers, colleagues, and peers. The most effective leaders offer everyone individual attention—especially if they are members of their work team.

Do you believe that individual treatment is important? Old school management scoffed at this idea, treating anyone who worked with others as "soft." Modern leaders recognize that individual treatment is essential for anyone who influences others. People want to be understood as unique in their actions and thoughts. Transformational leaders invest time and attention in understanding people, and react uniquely to them. When a great leader offers authentic individual consideration, people feel that they are understood and appreciated. John Maxwell wrote, "People don't care how much you know, until they know how much you care." Transformational leaders do care, and others discover this quickly.

In the next chapter, we will consider two important questions: How does one intentionally prepare for a career change? What do we know about leadership related to a career change?

LESSONS FOR LEADERS

Being a leader means that you will be more effective with other people. People will listen to you and watch what you are doing.

How do you influence people to do things now? Is the quality of your relationship important? Or do you rely on the authority you have been given as a manager or owner of a business?

Increasingly, show people that they are important to you. Build depth to your relationships through listening and trust. If you have the power to influence others, you may not need the power to give commands.

Chapter 5 - The Intentional Career Change

Your career change should not be an accident. Stumbling into the next phase of your career would be disastrous, as the changes may not be positive. However, much of forward planning seems like a fool's quest. We are not completely free to create our future. Learning about how work feels for you may lead to a different emotional experience than you had hoped to find.

Woody Allen wrote, "If you want to make God laugh, tell him about your plans." As we step forward, we must dance and adapt to the complex world we discover. Planning is helpful, especially as it prepares the mind for changes. However, the career changer often must improvise. Life surprises all of us. Plans help us to arrange the resources and consider the contingencies. A career explorer must build new factors into one's effort.

Some people resist adapting their strategy. Many things change. A plan too carefully plotted can restrict one from making better choices. The horizon moves forward to meet the career changer, in the face of surprise; one must be ready to strike out in a new direction. A career changer can preserve his or her intentions, even when he or she modifies plans. If one intends to "launch a marketing business which achieves $3 million in sales," the intention can follow the transitioner even as the plans are scrubbed. Intentions can endure. Intentions are like an arrow pointing in a direction.

It is said that a commercial jet makes dozens of course corrections over a routine flight. Much of the time, the jet is not pointed in the right direction. With the intention to reach the destination, a pilot and professional team guides the vessel to the correct airport and gate. The intention does not change, even while the flight plans face regular adjustment.

> **DR. STEVE'S TIPS FOR LEADERS**
>
> Chances are good that you are considering a course correction to your life. This may be a great time to affirm something bigger than yourself. Work on something with passion.
>
> Take a look at what you value. What is SO important to you that you would be willing to work many extra hours without being paid well? Understand your own value system, and let this push you forward.
>
> If you live by clear values, and you consistently encourage others to do the same, you will be seen as a leader by others who do not have this clarity.
>
> Paint your life in refreshing new terms. This is a great time to become a leader!

HOW DOES ONE MAKE AN INTENTIONAL CAREER TRANSITION?

An intentional career change proceeds through four phases. These are the vision phase, the research phase, the action phase, and the persistence (or continuance) phase. A career changer may move through some of these phases quickly, and move through other phases so slowly that the period seems endless. A single phase may have several meaningful milestones. Individual experiences always vary.

THE VISION PHASE

The vision phase is a preliminary part of the career change, where an individual contemplates the change, and imagines the endpoint. In the story, *The Wizard of Oz,* Dorothy had a vision of the Emerald City. Although a vision may not be clearly seen by a career changer, the person contemplating a change likely inserts an imaginary landscape of the destination. The vision is inspired by problems with the current situation; the destination is a place where these problems are resolved. The vision can inspire any person toiling with challenges to move ahead, because the picture reassures one that better things are ahead.

In the vision phase, one is not committed toward action. The experience of the vision fills many with delight, while some are not sure that they are worthy of their goal. The competing interest of job security creates a push-pull sensation. A career changer may feel pulled forward by the sweetness of the vision, yet pushed back by the security of the past career. Vision holds one's attention, and then the nervous realization that the route forward is not known causes many career changers to focus again on security.

What is the range of your vision? You may not have a scale of time attached to your vision. Make a decision that your vision will be realized, and include a definite date. As you add detail, such as time, your mind works harder to make the vision a reality. In the book *Psycho-Cybernetics*, Maxwell Maltz described the subconscious mind as a goal-seeking mechanism. Detail helps to inform the mind about the firmness of your intention.

Treat your vision as a fragile flower that needs protection. Not everyone will respect your vision – for your own well-being, be careful who learns about your vision. At the same time, you should connect to your vision. Absorb the idea of your vision fully; try it on your emotional self. Make sure that you understand how the vision will change your life. The connection with your vision is important for your coming journey through career change.

Do not reveal the vision too early to others, until you have absorbed the meaning of the future state in your life. At some point you will need to discuss the vision broadly; however, the vision may need to mature internally while you grow comfortable with the impact on your future life. The vision deserves a chance to build its own logic, structure, and flexibility. A vision may develop into a compelling force, if allowed to mature. You are the greenhouse that gives an important vision a chance to take root.

A vision matures by adding connections to real life. As you move closer to fulfillment, your vision will become invested with your life energy. The context of your life, and the possibilities that you work for, will come to reflect the potential of your vision. Connections anchor the vision to the dynamics of the world. When you follow the intentional direction of the vision, the eye of possibility finds new opportunities to make dreams crystallize into reality. Move forward and your dream can become a compelling force for its own manifestation. You may discover strategies to change your world as you focus on the dream. You are not the master of your vision, but you may become its primary advocate.

What support will your vision require? As you move in the direction of your dream, the vision may push you beyond the realm of comfort and toward a place where your foothold is tentative. Look for support after your vision has matured within you. Learn to trust that others will support your vision if you are authentic and emotionally resonant in your approach.

When you have a mature vision, look for strategies that expand its implementation. Consider options – how will this vision express itself? You carry the potential blossoming of this ideation into form and structure. If the vision is robust with possibility, you can express the vision through multiple routes. Look for richness; explore the possibilities. Articulate the multiple strategies in writing. If the vision makes the world a better place, you may discover that you have an ethical responsibility to help the vision achieve a concrete form.

THE RESEARCH PHASE

The vision phase of career change precedes action. Before one launches into committed effort, conduct research into the route ahead. Research before a career change includes clarification about one's own talents and strengths, as well as looking at the context of the new work. Be an informed sojourner. Explore yourself and the world you are moving toward before you advance into action.

What are your career strengths? Marcus Buckingham, author of *Go Put Your Strengths to Work* (2007), teaches people to learn about their strengths. Knowledge of career strengths may help a leader work with energy, produce better work, achieve greater results, and continue working while others feel fatigued. Knowledge of strengths is a valuable resource as one plans a journey forward.

Learn about your strengths. Look at the work that you perform, and consider how to change your emotional state when you work on different tasks. Some work will lift your spirits, other work can drain you. Take notes on the work, the conditions around your labor, and the change in your energy level. This knowledge can help you move out of your current situation and receive the results you want. If you make good choices, you may spend more time working on tasks in your strengths area.

Clarify your strategies. Your strategies for career change will be the major actions that you take to reach your vision. Understand clearly what course you will be taking. Build a map for your journey.

As you have spent some time working on your strengths, you will be able to apply yourself in a meaningful way. Build your strategies on your strengths and your values. Determine in advance where your focus will be. The strategic view will help to determine your allocation of resources, including your time.

Connect your strategies to your resources. Anticipate the time that you will need to implement your effort. Do you have a budget for your strategies? Consider adding in a 20% contingency budget to help you support your strategic efforts. You may need more time or material than you had imagined. Listen to your informed sources.

Having identified your strategies, and having reviewed your resources, look to the tactics that you will employ. The tactics are the actions that support your strategies in your career change. Each strategy may require a number of tactical actions. Tactics are the day-to-day plans that advance one's strategy.

Over time, you will need to revise your tactics. Scrutinize your tactics with the perspective gained as you begin working on your change. The tactics may have to be adapted, however the bigger picture – your strategy – should remain stable. Design your tactics to help you get started, but stay flexible with future actions that you pursue.

Why plan on a set of tactics, if they are subject to change? Because a leader prepares his or her mind for the new situation, and the career changer studies tactics in advance. Committing tactics in writing, planning in one's mind, and comparing resources to the challenges ahead help one sharpen perceptions and develop the ready mind. This ready mind can help you to conquer. Think tactically before you act, and be ready to drop specific choices if they become irrelevant. The prepared mind should treat tactical choices as options for action, not as committed efforts.

Suppose that you are starting a limousine business. You hope to capture a share of the airport, celebrity, sport events, and business travel in your community. Express this business in strategic goals. You will then work on a number of tactics to help you get there. You may have a financial partner who will help you lease or purchase your vehicles. You may work on building a network of connections with hotels, resorts, event planners, and catering businesses. In addition, you will plan a printed brochure, a website, and rack cards for destinations. You will establish maintenance and cleaning programs for your deluxe vehicles. Each of these tactics will help you reach your strategic goals, but you may have to adapt your tactics to suit your resources and immediate needs.

Set up timelines for your tactics. When doing your research, think about what steps will need to be accomplished before another tactic can begin. Some tactics may depend on completion in another area.

As you prepare your tactics for a change, consider your own readiness. "Most people are rather casual about preparation until the warnings begin in earnest" (Prochaska, Norcross, DiClemente, 1994, p. 45). Make your career change intentionally. Include the changes that you will pursue in the way you work. Reflect on how you might improve your actions in the future. Begin the change process with the intention of readiness in all that you do.

Establish a guiding question. A guiding question is an internal challenge that helps you direct your thinking toward the future. With a number of unknown factors to process, the guiding question can help you focus on important choices and discard distractions. If you are planning to open a financial services firm, perhaps your question will be, "How am I uniquely qualified to help my clients?" The question will direct your thinking to sharpen your working strengths, and help you tell your story to your clients. A guiding question may help you allocate limited resources better. While in the research stage, develop a guiding question to challenge you. The question may act as an internal mentor, prodding you to achieve your best.

The guiding question can help you to say "yes" and "no" to various alternatives. When you find that you are uncertain about the right choice, turn to your guiding question. Pause, and listen. Your quest for answers and knowledge of your vision can help you focus on what is important. The posture of questioning keeps your mind open to alternatives.

Do you have experts that can help you advance your research? Spend time with someone who has some knowledge of your journey; offer to take that person to lunch. Extend trust and prepare to learn about your career sojourn. Prepare for this meeting by drawing up important questions in advance–fill this time with purpose. Invest in planning for your expert contact time. Explore your vision with someone you trust, and in periods of private reflection. Make yourself ready to take bolder steps forward.

A set of experts, personally chosen, can help you advance faster and avoid points of danger. Your expert team can act like a mastermind group, designed to provide you intellectual depth for your journey forward. Let your expert team review your research and strategic plans before you launch.

Collect the information that will help you advance through your career change. With a guiding question, knowledge of your strengths, a strategic plan, and advice from experts, you can make the best use of your time. Understand that you will never be able to end the flood of information if you keep searching in a well-prepared state. Look for the information that you need. Explore worthwhile leads.

Prepare to end your research at some reasonable point. For some people, the collection of worthwhile information can be so enticing that it is hard to end. Research information is valuable to you only when you have a chance to continue to action.

THE ACTION PHASE

Several days ago, I drove to another city. I depended on my map to get there. En route, I discovered that a shorter route existed, a route that was much more convenient for me. My map helped me; however, I deviated from my planned route. Do not be afraid to make course deviations off your map if you receive information. Stay flexible, and remain open to learn more from your journey. Route changes are allowed!

Once you have your map, ready yourself for action. Set a date for action. Follow your map. Look ahead as you approach any milestone; consider the terrain that you have covered. Be proud of the progress you have made toward a goal, because your goal may deepen the value of your life. Your map will help you fix a steady effort toward the vision of a positive career change. Know what your next steps will be.

Allow yourself the freedom to improvise. You have already explored the route ahead, and conducted research as you best can. Your mind is prepared for the challenges, so if you notice a better route, do so consciously. If you are aware of your map, you will not make blind turns that compromise your advance.

Your map will not alert you to all the obstacles you face. Consider your choices. You might try a detour around big problems.

Your experience and research will help you. The experts you have contacted earlier may guide you when you face an unexpected challenge. Perhaps your experience with the obstacle will help set you up as an expert in your new life.

All leaders face challenges; a leader's history of achievement, combined with the courage to continue forward, inspires other followers. Hard challenges are part of the life education of a leader. The experience gained helps one continue effort throughout life; lesser challenges may slow others down. The leader with proven experience may approach confidently as other tests appear.

Measure your progress regularly. Review the accomplishments that you have made as you move forward. Recognize that significant effort goes into creating a new career. Enjoy a satisfying pause as you recognize that you have met challenges and prevailed. Do your emotions move you to doubt your progress? I know that I have felt negative emotions dominate me for days at a time. I have learned that I can manage my emotions and be productive with my efforts. My decision-making and action-taking mind does not need to take orders from my emotional core.

Some emotions give us energy. Others leave us weakened. The positive emotions may not create a barrier for us – in fact, they may inspire us to work harder! However, the negative emotions can leave us feeling drained when we need to take bold action for our careers. Manage your activities even when your emotions pull you away from your purpose.

If an emotion slows you down, take a good look at it. Do not deny the emotional reality, as the chances are good that a suppressed emotion may come back even stronger in another way. Understand the negative feeling. Get to know its emotional logic.

Do all you can to step forward. Understand that your negative emotion will not last forever. Your investment in time and effort in pushing forward may even change your emotional state. Recognize your emotions and move forward. Emotions change regularly.

THE CONTINUANCE, OR PERSISTENCE PHASE

As you manage your emotions, you may have entered the persistence phase. As you have explored your vision, completed your research, and taken action steps toward your better life, you may now be continuing your efforts until you reach milestones. The persistence phase may be a period where you allow *no excuses* to interfere with your progress. During the persistence period, your dreams are still on the horizon or beyond. You should not worry about having made the wrong choices in the persistence phase, as you have prepared yourself perfectly for this position. To move beyond the persistence phase, keep up your efforts. Take all reasonable actions, and remain of good cheer!

Continuing forward makes you lucky. Keep working on the career tasks that you identified in your plan. Each push forward is like a new roll of the dice. Be grateful that you have a chance to express your abilities, and the universe may bless you in ways that you never anticipated.

Follow your vision. Your soul calls for the better life you have seen. "It does not matter how slowly you go, as long as you do not stop," said Confucius. Going slowly forward is much better than stopping! Honor the psychic investment in your dream, and gain by inches until you have a breakthrough. Be your own representative for the future; others will notice and credit you for your decision to achieve a big success.

Scan the horizon, and look for opportunities. You create your own advantage by focusing on your destiny, and finding compatible platforms to advance your interest. Stay aware of your purpose. While you should have a flexible outlook toward new opportunities, do not chase detours. Every investment of your professional effort should support your strategic choices. Some of us are distractible, and the allure of easy money can divert us from our noble purpose. Your time and resources should fertilize the vision that you have already seen.

The resources that you have collected so far will help you make the journey. Your map, your expert sources, your strategies, and the energy that you bring to this venture can help you renew in small stages. Recently, I turned to one of the sources that helped me as I prepared my personal journey, and discovered exactly the wisdom to help me improve my work. Your review could help you find a nugget of wisdom that you had forgotten.

THE NEUTRAL ZONE

William Bridges writes about transitions, and describes the journey exceedingly well. He calls the middle phase of transition the "neutral zone" (2008). In the neutral zone, one is not connected to the past or the future, and intentions are easily shifted back and forward. Somewhere, the career changer must find the internal resources, the energy, and the will to push toward his or her vision. The neutral zone has its dangers. Without fortitude, the career changer may stall out, and abandon the vision. The vision, the map, and personal determination are allies to help the career changer continue until he or she reaches milestones.

When the career changer pushes forward without touching success, it is natural to experience anxiety. The inner critic may speak up, quashing motivation to move forward. In spite of continued somber feelings, the career changer should resolve to follow one's vision and achieve the next milestone.

Accompanying anxiety, the career changer may experience the weak parts of one's working life. We all have relative strengths and weaknesses in the way that we work. While the career changer is in the neutral zone, he or she feels weaknesses acutely. Don't identify with the weaknesses, simply follow the business plan. With weaknesses and strengths, one can still follow a well-prepared plan.

We strive to see results for our efforts. During this period, an emerging leader lays the foundations for future success. If you are in the neutral zone and feel overloaded with work, review your work. The neutral zone is a dangerous area for one's dreams. Few of us succeed in reaching our goals without the help and support of other people, the circle of colleagues we trust with the treasure of our dreams and hopes. During the crossing of the neutral zone, our allies likely will see our reluctance that comes from being between a safe haven and a destination named in a vision. Tell your friends that you are changing your career, and your dream has not changed. Ask for a lift of energy. Return to your action plan as quickly as possible.

The neutral zone is also a period of creative opportunity. When circumstances look uncertain, you may be attuned to see the career change with a fresh perspective. Continue learning about your new career, and invest new energy into gaining the vocabulary of a practitioner in the work you are about to enter. Shift your thinking so that you can think *as if* you have already reached your milestones.

Don't sabotage your own power. Our mind directs us to do wonderful things, but many of us hold thoughts that pull down our energy. Do you ever hear negative self-talk, words running through your mind that tell you, "I am not worthy of this," or, "This is never going to happen"?

Be glad that you have recognized the critic in your own mind. Instead of feeding this part of you, focus on your plan. Replace negativity with a positive resolve. Instead of saying, "Shut up!" to your voice of negativity, add positive self-talk. Struggle does not help you with negativity, and it may add energy to the dark side.

Be glad of your own power, and visualize your journey toward the big dream. Focus on the positive things that bring your vision into reality. Your positive self-talk can be an energizing tool to help you past challenges.

Consider the mental shifts that help you reach your vision. You may need to change your thinking and adopt new frameworks of understanding that reflect your new view of the world. In the neutral zone, you have loosened the ties with your old career, but they are not yet broken. You may need to change your thinking before your milestones and major success happen. This period of neutrality is an excellent time to think *as if* the future were nearby. Think playfully and with possibilities in mind. Stretch your mind ahead to your future self, the career changer who has reached the opposite shore. Your way of thinking must expand and shift.

On the inside of the neutral zone, you may be adjusting your thinking, accommodating the reality of your future. To you, the new framework appears as a needed expansion to fit your new world. Both perspectives are useful. Take the next step toward your vision, and new ideas may emerge without struggle.

All bets are off in the neutral zone. Use the potential power of the space to innovate. All things are possible in the neutral zone, if enough directed effort follows. Take risks that point you toward the goal. Try new ways of working.

The neutral zone is a good place to redefine yourself. Between a secure job and an uncertain future, career changers can reevaluate their priorities. In this phase, do you still think of your future career as "work"? Perhaps you will need a new mental model, one that gives you the flexibility to commit more energy in a playful way toward your new career. Look to your vision, and understand that your career efforts may be quite different in your new phase. "Play" might be a better model, or perhaps "service" can represent your life efforts in the next phase of your career. Be willing to change how you think of your working hours. If you are going to expand your circle of performance, that word, "work," may no longer be sufficient to describe your new kind of life.

Change your metaphor. Let that metaphor change guide you as you make new decisions. You may earn your right to claim your new career by seeing and serving in new ways. A career change may depend on your expanded view of the effort you offer to life.

To become a leader of men and women, you may need to make your professional activities an opportunity to change people's lives. Work is something that you may continue to do, with toil and labor remaining the mundane part of your efforts. Changing lives is a leadership effort, one that will mark you as a nearly magical member of your community.

EMERGING AS A LEADER

As a leader, you may be a servant, you may be a change agent, and you may have special experience. The leader conducts many selfless acts in favor of others. If your focus as a leader is, "When do I get mine?" then your rewards will be limited. In the next section, we will explore what some respected sources have said about leadership, and consider how their ideas might be applied to career change. Leaders sometimes manage change, and leaders often initiate change. The work of leadership guides people through change. An effective leader must understand how to improvise, and how to deal with uncertainty. These skills are important for career changers, although not all establish themselves as leaders.

Do you feel that the role of a leader is to shoulder a large burden? A good leader has an expansive sense of caring and responsibility, and many talented people prefer defined limits to their authority. In my experience, a good leader often has other people assign new areas of responsibility because of the leader's effective handling of other issues. Naturally, some people prefer to avoid extra responsibilities. The growing leader will often experience unexpected new responsibilities.

Career changers may not intend it; however, they may be unintentionally preparing themselves as leaders. The experience of shifting careers may be one of the best life challenges to teach a leader.

> **LESSONS FOR LEADERS**
>
> Use this time of career change to change the way you view the world. Change your metaphor for working.
>
> What is your metaphor right now? Are you a "loyal employee" or a "captain of your team?" When you are inventing a new career, your metaphor may need to change. Notice the way you think about your work.

Chapter 6 - The Work of a Leader

*I've been on that bridge. There ain't
no rails on that bridge.*
~ Comment by a career-changer

THE WORK OF A LEADER

What do leaders do?

Most of this book examines the work of leaders by talking to people who have become leaders in their new careers, and by discussing the ideas of scholars and opinion leaders. This chapter starts by turning to published authors, recognized for their contribution to the field of leadership. The views of leadership scholars are often built on the experience of their work and contact with business, government, non-profit, and artistic leaders. The next chapter will consider leadership myths. If you would rather skip these ideas, simply turn to chapter 8.

> ### DR. STEVE'S TIPS FOR LEADERS
> Being a leader takes work! You may need to change your relationship with people and results. The journey of a leader is uniquely personal for everyone.

FIVE PRACTICES OF LEADERS

In their work on *The Leadership Challenge* (2002), Kouzes and Posner name five actions of leaders. All leaders a) model the way,

b) inspire a shared vision, c) challenge the process, d) enable others to act, and e) encourage the heart.

MODEL THE WAY

Modern career changers include entrepreneurs and solopreneurs. When I ask, "Are you a leader?" I am often told "I don't have any employees, how can I be a leader?" New business leaders may not directly control other people; however, they may still demonstrate a bold choice that other people will follow. When an entrepreneur inspires others to copy him, leadership is present. People follow leaders because leaders model a new way of working.

A leader's model can also include a mental attitude and an approach to thinking about the problem. Followers may learn from the leader how to evaluate the situation and choose an action. Leaders often offer a nuanced guide to acting in the face of uncertainty. Models are an indicator of leadership. People follow leaders. The leader's good example may move people to action.

A SHARED VISION

Leaders add vision to raw possibility. They add insight and positive thinking to an unstructured space, and create value.

I describe "vision" as, "The ability to apply experience to possibilities." .

Leaders provide the power of directed imagination to the challenges of work and society. The visioning process is a creative act, one that applies evaluation of the facts, a review of the assumptions, and the work of applied inquiry to explore the applications of vision to practical needs. Providing the visioning work, leaders make possible blueprints, contracts, and specification lists. The work of visioning anticipates the physical labor connected with fulfillment of the big vision.

By sharing their vision, leaders unite people to create something new and wonderful.

CHALLENGE THE PROCESS

Like entrepreneurs, leaders are willing to do things in a new way. People in career transition have this quality in common with leaders. They challenge the process. The career changer looks for new activities of work and results. The career changer may be working for an important new purpose.

A leader is aware of the purpose behind a change. People support a process change only when there is greater value to be created. Career changers may be moved by an opportunity or because of work dissatisfaction, and they see the value ahead. Challenging the system requires a high level of determination and effort. Career changers act like leaders when they push against the inertia of past work habits and complacent routines.

Our life structures keep us anchored to a familiar *beat* of working. Leadership occurs when one resists the familiar and creates a new cycle of effort and outcomes. The determined career changer must work on a new pattern for months before new processes become familiar and background to the big picture. If one persists in a new process, new habits are strengthened which define the career and support a leadership perspective.

LEADERS ENABLE OTHERS TO ACT

A leader is not a solo artist! True leaders work with other people, not just with a job, but also with volunteers and people influenced. Leadership is more than self-discipline and artistic expression. Leaders influence other people.

The attention of a leader makes a difference with other people. A leader encourages and authorizes followers to perform, sometimes independently. Followers are energized by a caring leader who notices their work. Even if their relationship is not as a boss and worker, a leader can influence others. As a result of this caring attention, people in the circle of the leader feel empowered to act.

Career changers may help others to act by bringing their earlier career experiences forward. Even unrelated experience may suggest a challenge to a new situation. A career changer who has embraced the uncertainty of change may have a useful perspective for a problem in another setting. Even the mind of the career changer, broadened by new experiences, may offer energizing information for followers in a new setting.

The career changer may be a solo entrepreneur, and still enable others to act. One of the qualities of a leader is that he or she connects with an expanded range of colleagues. A leader might even be a direct competitor, and offer guidance for a colleague in another business. The impact of a leader bursts organizational charts. People seek out help from a good leader no matter where he or she works. The guidance of an effective leader will be sought by friends and interested parties.

Of the many actions of a leader, perhaps attention and appreciation are the two acts that enable people to act with greatest confidence. Leaders energize others with their attention. Positive appreciation helps others feel that their actions will contribute. Leaders carry gravitas with their thoughts and words. After a leader expresses appreciation, others feel that they have been positively reviewed, and that hope is on their side. As the leader speaks, others feel that they have a great chance for success, because the leader has endorsed their plan. The attention of the leader is like an endorsement, and people may find their spirit lifted because of the leader's approval.

ENCOURAGE THE HEART

Leaders connect to the heart. Their words are weighted with experience. When a leader provides insight on the road ahead, followers feel that the challenge is smaller. The leader has personal insight into the challenges that others face. When the leader offers hope, followers judge the insight to be authentic help.

Kouzes wrote that one consistent quality found in leaders is that they have been significantly challenged in their careers. Tough times, followed by action and fortunate choices, lead to personal growth. Leaders have experienced working on the edge of their performance, and have given their personal best. Their words to a follower will offer sincere hope, created from vivid life experience and pain.

Not only do leaders have the capacity to encourage the heart, but I have found that most are driven to help others. They encourage others with the hope that followers will not feel the pain and change that the leader went through. Leaders draw on their pain and joy earned from life experience.

People thrive on encouragement. A few simple words of positive attention may lift a person's energy level for hours. In my volunteer work with Toastmasters, I have seen people work hard for months, drive across the state, attend countless meetings, and spend their own money on projects because someone has encouraged them. More than once, I have heard a leader say, "Bill noticed me. He predicted I would be my club's president, and it came true." Well-chosen words can change someone's life.

We can live without encouragement for some time, but we cannot live well. Encouragement may not be missed until a severe case of despair hits a person. Tough-minded, achievement-oriented people may not state their need for encouragement, but they appreciate it when they get it! If are working hard, you may need words of encouragement. Leaders refresh the working soul. If you are following a big purpose, a leader may help you sustain your effort. Leaders encourage the heart.

HOW DO LEADERS ENCOURAGE THE HEART?

Leaders make a personal connection with their followers, and through an authentic relationship, that connection is felt deeply. This power to move others deeply at a purposeful and emotional level is perhaps the greatest leader ability.

Leaders are often in the position of recognizing the contribution of their followers. Small-minded managers sometimes denigrate their direct reports, or steal credit for work well done. A great leader makes sure that the follower gets the credit. Other followers know the superior leader to be fair-minded and generous with recognition.

Followers receive appreciation from leaders, even when their work is not completed. The warm spirit of a leader notices other people performing well, and often states so publicly. This gift of appreciation translates into encouragement of the heart.

Leaders make it official: *Celebrate the victories.* The influential leader offers time, place, and opportunities for followers to publicly honor their successes. A leader offers the official benediction that makes the celebration memorable. Leaders offer small and large celebrations to honor their followers for the spirit of their contribution.

Through appreciation, recognizing efforts, and celebrations, leaders build community. Followers and leaders come to enjoy working together or sharing experiences. The social motive is a powerful link between people of a common purpose. Even leaders who work independently find reason to connect people as community. Communities sustain themselves, and they tend to generate stories, heroes, and even new leaders. When a leader has encouraged enough hearts to build a community, the members of the group will find reasons to work with the leader on new ventures.

CAREERS BY CHOICE

The classical concept of a strong business included three foundations: capital, management, and labor. Assembly lines required managers who could keep workers in line. The knowledge of an organization resided in both managers and workers; however, managers understood both the strategic direction of the company and the business processes that made the company profitable. Workers could be exchanged, and others could be trained.

In the twenty-first century, the importance of workers has risen, and the importance of managers, especially middle-managers, has declined. When an experienced employee leaves, much of the knowledge of the company leaves as well. The value of the worker has increased, especially compared with the manager.

A career is valued because of what one knows. A worker with specialized knowledge can negotiate with a larger business on the terms of work. A knowledge worker, one whose value is driven by special knowledge, frequently works as an independent consultant, refusing to accept narrow terms of employment. The person who continually invests in new knowledge, and builds career experience, has an opportunity to drive the conditions for work.

We have the opportunity now to learn, work, and prepare our careers for new results. We can consciously create a new career. Our knowledge is the foundation for a new career.

This age of rapid change has created many paradoxes. Changes come with technology and with the way business is conducted globally. An individual with leadership talent and awareness of new possibilities can create new enterprise. The presence of change confuses some, but also opens opportunities for entrepreneurs and alert leaders to fill needs in new ways.

If you are changing careers, make your selection consciously. Study the emerging markets created by new technology, and listen to the unmet needs of the people in your circles. Use your knowledge and talent to choose your next career.

> **LESSONS FOR LEADERS**
>
> *When you become a leader, the eyes of your colleagues and friends will be on you. Everyone will be watching what you say and do. You are always modeling the way forward. Don't get overwhelmed, but do be aware — people notice what you are doing. If you are inconsistent, people will see that, faster than you might imagine.*
>
> *Once you think about the consequences of your actions as a leader, the impact can be personally staggering. Be responsible; you are changing the world. Leadership is about love.*

Chapter 7 - Examine Leadership Myths

Pursue your personal vision. With this strategy alone, the career-changer starts acting like a leader. Without even seeking a leadership role, career-changers start something important that influences how other people work. In the pursuit of a worthwhile outcome, a career-changer may lead others. Leaders are often borne of necessity.

In my doctorate research, I talked to a number of teachers who denied that they were leaders in their school. Many teachers resist school administration, sometimes despising the roles. Not everyone wants to be seen as a leader. I heard from many teachers who had a a confrontational attitude toward school leaders. Some teachers see school leaders as "the enemy."

I could have an interesting discussion with teachers about the role of a leader. The way I view leaders, the leader is a person of influence, not simply a person who wields authority. Bennis and Nanus, authors of *Leaders* (2003), identified commonly held views about leaders, and stipulated five myths about the role. These myths may be instructive to career-changers. If you are consciously creating your future, you may be dancing in the nether world between dreamer and leader. Not sure if you want to be a leader?

MYTH: LEADERSHIP IS A RARE SKILL

Many people act as leaders. Leadership happens whenever a person chooses to act in a new direction, and influences other people. Although many people can act as leaders, this does not mean that everyone is a *great* leader.

> **DR. STEVE'S TIPS FOR LEADERS**
> Challenge your myths.
>> Move ahead with what you believe.
>> Leadership is not a rare skill.
>> Leaders are made; it is an intentional and lifelong process.
>> Your charisma will not qualify you as a leader, though the charisma can fool some people.
>> You can act as a leader right where you are—you don't need to be a CEO.
>> Great leaders use the power of influence, not control and manipulation.

Leaders may not act like others expect them to. They may not support the same politics or vision as others. Don't look for a good leader to support your cause, no matter how righteous its purpose. Instead, leaders follow their own vision.

It is possible that you have missed noticing good leaders in your world. More people may serve as leaders than you credit. Although exceptional leaders may be rare, you may have a number of people around you who act as leaders at least some of the time.

I encourage you to start noticing the leadership potential in other people. If you treat people as leaders, they may rise to your expectations.

MYTH: LEADERS ARE BORN

We may not be perfect; however, leadership is something that can be made of us. Leadership is a quality borne of challenging experiences, reflection, and action. Leaders have given of their sweat and blood to become who they are. The formation of a leader is a lifelong achievement. Warren Bennis said that leaders are continuous learners throughout their life.

Career-changers may start a journey of personal transformation that prepares them for leadership. The purpose for many career-changers may be to create a more satisfying life, and leadership may not be the intention. Our travel defines us, regardless; leadership skill is a by-product of certain experiences. Through the fire of life challenges, career-changers and entrepreneurs follow the leader's curriculum.

Have you said, "I'm not a leader?" You may not have been born a leader, neither are the people who influenced you. You may have started down the leader's journey with your career change, a transformation that will never be completed as long as you are still learning.

MYTH: LEADERS ARE CHARISMATIC

The charismatic person attracts followers. Bennis tells us, however, that most leaders are not charismatic; they are ordinary. Neither good looks, artistic talents, nor a dazzling personality are sufficient qualities of leaders. Attraction is not the same as leadership. To influence a person over a sustained period, a leader must offer something of substance.

The powers of charisma are useful for a leader. However, the powers of attraction may limit a leader's ability to transmit powerful ideas. If the follower focuses on the face, smile, or vocal tone of the leader, the important message may get lost. Leaders change people from the inside out.

I believe that the best leaders act as servants, not as rock stars. Although some leaders hold a nearly hypnotic power over followers, such power of attraction is limited and fickle. The sustaining power of a leader is the authentic relationship with others who share a compelling vision.

The glamour of a superficial leader can be tarnished. When a leader is discovered to be flawed, a trust bond may be permanently severed. The leader who promotes the importance of the mission over his or her personal role is immune from bad news and another charismatic replacement leader. Accordingly, put more effort into recognizing followers and sharing value, as these qualities cannot be eclipsed by changing times.

MYTH: LEADERSHIP CAN OCCUR ONLY AT THE TOP

Good leaders work in all levels of an organization. The senior people may have followers without loyalty, while front-line workers may be experienced, practical leaders. Leadership is not a measure of organizational rank. Leaders can influence people whatever their position.

Effective people do rise in organizations, and leadership is an indicator of effectiveness. Leaders will migrate to the top of their organizations because they make a difference. Leaders may also leave an organization to work for another, or start their own business. Change is part of the leadership context, and leaders tend to rise by their efforts. A smart career-changer will look for the signs of a leader anywhere in the organization. A visionary career-changer can enlist supporters who believe in the dream, and act as leaders in helping the idea form as a realistic business achievement.

Leadership is relevant at any level of a workplace. Look beyond job title. Look to the quality of the character and the nimbleness of the mind. Leaders are often the masters of a changing situation.

MYTH: LEADERS CONTROL, DIRECT, AND MANIPULATE

This myth carries forward an unfortunate, old-school image of leaders. Great leaders connect people. The leaders for our age of change and innovation use social influence and authentic relationships instead of the powers of control to get the best out of their teams. Knowledge workers tire of taking orders from tyrants.

Transformative leaders use the talents of their followers to create results. Transformation demands engagement, and engagement does not come from a manipulative relationship. People like to be connected by a leader who displays authentic caring and emotional intelligence. Any leader who employs a lot of manipulation will face resistance from employees. The power of control ends as soon as the controls are turned off.

The effective leader uses encouragement, words of affirmation, and the interests of the follower to build a sustained connection with the leader's purpose. Leaders and career-changers work toward a meaningful goal. The powers of command and control are not strong enough to capture the imagination, hearts, and souls of hard-working people. People disconnect from control and manipulation as soon as they can. A leader can offer meaning to followers who want their labor to count for something. If you are a career-changer looking to enlist followers, find a way to sell the big picture.

THE LEADERSHIP WELL

The well is a gathering place for a community, and a source where a pilgrim can draw nourishing water. Because of the value to the community, people often congregate. All the neighbors draw their vital life force from this source. No one remembers how deep the well is, no one remembers who built the well, and the well's bottom has never been plumbed within recent memory. Peering down, one gazes into a mysterious depth, which is dark and contains unknown elements.

Where do leaders get their vision and experience? Look down the well. Do you see your reflection?

Drinking deeply, the leader remembers teams hired and fired, business plans funded and discarded, the thrill of a bold new venture, and the voices of people in pain. A leader somewhere launched a new computer, led a rescue team in Central America, and built a hospital in Africa. The leader's previous life is the well. Pull deep. A leader may be able to draw lessons about change and people from the lives of other leaders in his teaching lineage.

Rita was a nurse, a mother, and a skilled businessperson; she inspired me. She is my well. She taught me how to appreciate differences in people, showed me how to have patience with others, and always affirmed my special contribution to our work. I found confidence in her treatment of me. When I am not sure how to proceed, part of me asks, "What would Rita do?" Even though she has been deceased for two decades, her inspiring words remain with me as I act.

The well is more than a conscience. It is a source of experience. If you have worked with a mentor, been influenced by a great man or woman, or been stirred by the actions of Ghandi or Martin Luther King Jr., you have a well that you can draw upon. Have a moment of doubt? Pause and refresh. Draw from the well. Reflect on what you might learn from personal experience or the lives of others.

What does your well look like? Rita is one of the voices in my well; I have also called on the experience of three thought leaders to provide the source insight that I need. One of my sources is Carl Jung. I have read Jung's works for over four decades, and I have been impressed with his insight into the human condition and deep mysteries of life and spirit. He is a voice I imagine speaking to me. My connection is not metaphysical, merely conjectured.

Does Carl Jung's spirit still vibrate in the world, offering me insight and support? I am an agnostic on this position, open to the idea of influence at the spiritual level. Regardless, I have some appreciation for Jung's ideas. I can imagine what his views are. I ask this power, his voice, spirit, and insight to guide me. I leave it to others to decide if this is only a fantasy. If I am only imagining Jung's support, then I am engaging my creative power, drilling my well to a new level, based on the ideas of the Swiss psychologist. If my well is enriched by this cognitive exploration, I am satisfied by the result.

I dig my personal well with guidance from Rita and Carl Jung. I've also invited Leonardo da Vinci and George Harrison to be part of my leadership source, my well of knowledge. I invite all these historic people to help me make this a better world, one of the reasons for being a leader.

I prepare my well in quiet moments, respecting the insight that I know is available to me. As a leader, I know that my spirit will be tried. When I pause to meditate, when I seek new energy from my center, I find that my well is available to me throughout the day. I like to think I have activated a flow of sustenance that keeps me refreshed even while my frustration with the world drags me down. My well offers me reassurance that I am worthy, that I have many talents, that I am capable of meeting new challenges.

BUST THOSE MYTHS – DRAW ON YOUR OWN SOURCE OF KNOWLEDGE

Leaders are complex, social beings who enlist followers through the exchange of powerful ideas. The development of a leader may take years or decades. Career-changers may embark on the leadership journey through their challenges in building a business or through their new occupation.

Vision is important for leaders. Leaders deal with ideas and are usually superior at communicating them, often with stories. People around the leader come to understand the vision; sometimes the complexity and depth get revealed in stages. The clarity of the leader's vision is part of the leader's attraction to others.

Leaders cultivate a positive relationship with followers. Good leaders will make followers a priority in their attention. Leaders share ideas, recognition, and emotional experience. Some followers may become leaders themselves, with the assistance of the leader. A transmission of wisdom is often part of the leader-follower relationship. Leaders grow other leaders!

A leader's actions are marked by intention and conscious choice. In the face of confusion and anxiety, leaders are known to trust their inner resolve and vision of a better place. While a leader can benefit from happy accidents, a leader will choose a strategic direction consciously.

> **LESSONS FOR LEADERS:**
> *Think strategically.*
> *Don't be controlled by the myths of a cautious world.*
> *Move ahead as a leader, using the power of vision, positive relationships, and your conscious choices. You create your own opportunities.*

Chapter 8 - Connecting With Your People

A leader who needs to share a vision and launch a new enterprise will do this with the help of other people. Leadership is an art of achieving great things through the committed efforts of others. Leaders may start by themselves with an idea. The reach of a leader is greater than the power of a single person. If the power of a leader could be measured quantitatively, a high number of trusted connections would add gigawatts to the direct current of a single individual.

Leaders know their people. In a small business environment, a leader constantly expands his or her circle of influence. The business of networking involves establishing contact, sharing mutual opportunities of interest, and assessing potential for future business. Leaders make a priority of their time and attention to build knowledge of the people around them. Connecting with people is a smart investment in time.

> **DR. STEVE'S TIPS FOR LEADERS**
>
> Be a connector.
>
> Move people with ideas.
>
> Be responsible for your people.
>
> Promote your people.
>
> Get energized by the people around you.

I've been active in Toastmasters for over 20 years. I have seen how rapidly people can get connected to others. A new Toastmaster may meet twenty new people in her club. After speaking before the club three times, other members have a vivid impression of the interests and talents of their new colleague.

A Toastmaster that visits other clubs rapidly builds a circle of connections. By visiting just four other clubs in a period of six months, the member has the potential connection with an additional eighty people beyond the first circle. If he or she visits several times, the connections are stronger, and greater knowledge of talented people in the geographic community is rapidly expanded. Those hundred new contacts (20 people in five clubs) also know people. If the member graciously connects with people in all these clubs, his circle of influence will quickly grow beyond the people he has met, because friends know friends.

Successful career changers and emerging leaders connect with people. The connections built by achievers are usually rich experiences, meaningful to all parties. People in career transition find ways to enrich their relationships and create renewal while they are defining their life. Leaders understand that their ability to create change depends on the quality of human relationships. Connections are a bond between people that persist over time.

Why are these connections so meaningful and strong? Among the leaders I interviewed, the connection with others was the most frequently discussed factor. Connections provide a lift for the person making a change. However, there is mutuality in the experience; when an authentic connection is formed, the leader feels responsible for the other person's quality of life. Carl, a software entrepreneur, told me, "There came a moment when I realized the business momentum was not just about me, it was also about the people who worked for me. I had a responsibility to those people."

Career-changers told me that they consciously worked to expand their network. Friendships are not conquests. The people who emerged as leaders cared about their expanded circle. Other people are vitally important to them, no matter their calculated value to a new business enterprise.

A person in transition renews some neglected connections. Some friendships drift apart while life gets busy. The person in transition understands that all connections are important. In transition and beyond, the career-changer is energized by authentic emotional contact with colleagues. Even though the career-changer seeks interviews and information, sincere interest in the other person guides the process in a valued connection. If the bond was there before, the person in transition can often rekindle the connection by an honest effort.

The American writer, Ray Bradbury said, "We are cups, constantly and quietly being filled." Our inner life, our perceptions and rich experiences are delights to other people. Our differences and unique configuration of values are alien to many other people. To build a great connection, pour slowly. C. S. Lewis reveals that we all have the potential to make incredible breakthroughs in our connections when we risk enough to test barriers and offer substance from our inner life.

When the moment of "otherness" is overcome, people in transition expand their reach, building trusting relationships. Leaders in transition have shown me that our connections are a valuable life asset. Other people add value to life because of their independence and vital spirit. If the inner world is in tumult, it is hard to influence others.

True friendship comes when the silence between two people is comfortable. – **David Tyson Gentry**

POWER OF CONNECTIONS

The leader in transition becomes powerful through connections. I believe it is wrong to treat people as conquests, wrong to count people as a goal, as if a numerical score represents achievement. I know that the connected person has more opportunity to involve other people in big dreams. Connected people have more opportunity to lead, making a difference through people. Two factors surely influence the power of connections.

Number of connections. When a person strives to change careers, start a business, or launch a revolution, other people help make this happen. Connected people have more potential to collaborate with talented people. When the web of connections is large and diverse, the emerging leader has a great range of skills that might be accessed if needed.

Emotional intelligence. The power to influence other people varies between people. An emotionally intelligent person is self-aware and responsive in connection to others. The emotionally intelligent person is more persuasive, influences more people, and creates more value out of his or her connections than does the person with low emotional intelligence. Emotional intelligence assists any leader in transition with the power to skillfully connect with others. Some of the leader's connections become leaders in their own right, because they share a vision and enthusiasm with the leader, and act in support of a great purpose. Other people become centers of influence for a shared vision, and this connection can transform others into leaders themselves.

When more people follow a shared vision, the leader charges the network of connections with purpose. Some connected followers have the capacity to intensify and direct the energy of an authentic leader.

A VOICE FOR CONNECTION: JOHN C. MAXWELL

"Leaders are like locomotives in that they're blessed with drive, energy, and vision. However, until leaders learn the art of connection, their influence remains minimal," said writer and leadership expert John Maxwell. Maxwell has devoted many pages to the advantage of staying connected. He recommends that leaders get closer to their followers. Maxwell recommends that leaders take the initiative, and offer a plan for movement to followers. The leader's insight may be breathtaking – however, that insight may not be enough. Show your connections how they can get started, and contribute to the vision. Leaders will make a plan of action clear for others, offering a chance to apply action quickly. The leader helps other people get started in the face of fear, uncertainty, and anxiety. Leaders create a bridge to meaningful action.

Maxwell reminds leaders to find the key to action from connected friends. To do this, the leader invests time with every follower, engaging them in a personal dialogue about their values. The leader does not exploit this knowledge, instead shows others how their personal interests can advance in a powerful vision and plan of action.

NATHAN'S STORY

Nathan worked for a major specialty hospital in Philadelphia. He held the number two position in his department, and was responsible for the training and development of the nursing team, among other duties. He held professional licenses and degrees as a nurse, identified closely with the profession, and had begun to realize that he had substantial management and leadership talents. His vision of transforming his workplace, possibly transforming the work of nurses everywhere, began to burn in his soul as a major life purpose. Whenever Nathan spoke, I heard the optimism and powerful belief that he has for making nursing a more effective career choice.

At the same time, Nathan worked with a department head who pressed heavily with a sense of authority. The boss wanted results, and wanted Nathan to account for his time and effort on her terms. Nathan felt miserable under the tyranny that she presented.

The domination continually drained Nathan's vital spirits. He felt resilient whenever he worked closely with a nurse, and helped him or her become more effective. Nathan became a leader by virtue of a burning idea. Nathan wrote, trained, and spoke to colleagues about the humanizing force of nursing. He made friends in the human resources department, and in national associations.

Then Nathan's boss fired him. Even as Nathan emerged as a thought leader in his profession, the department head ended his position in the prestigious hospital. His platform for change ended even as he was building connections. Empowered nurses were not as manageable as self-directed ones.

Nathan could have applied for work with another specialty hospital. Nathan had a burning desire to lift the nursing profession. Even without a job, Nathan was well connected. He had touched many lives, spoken at conferences, and showed nurses that they could be more effective. Nathan's connections provided a launching pad to the next phase of his career.

Nathan came to understand that his career change was inevitable. He had emerged as a leader in his hospital, and in the greater nursing community. He had accepted a part-time teaching position, helping nurses receive their advanced education and credentials. He identified more and more with the work as a nurse leader and change agent. His heart had left his job with the hospital.

Relieved of his daily work, Nathan now faced the challenge of building a career without the support of steady employment and a regular paycheck. He went through his period of disorientation, and spoke to old connections. He continued to help nurses looking for career change, and he came to value his teaching position as a stable platform for him to offer other services. The credibility of a university position helped him expand his work as an independent provider of services.

Nathan followed his heart. He expanded his private work as a nurse career consultant, helping nurses to realize their purpose and clarify their skills and working strengths. He loves his new role and the ability to focus on building nurses' professional skills.

Nathan has taken a hit in his income, but his place as a leader continues to rise. No longer working with a secure job, Nathan defines the way he works in his unique personal way. He continues to make connections rapidly with nurses and health professionals around the country. His income directly follows his efforts, and he is busy creating products through books, newsletters, and training programs.

As I've talked to him, he sounds joyful as he finds new opportunities, working on a niche that he understands, supports, and passionately connects with the experience of his career journey.

LESSONS FROM CONNECTING

Nathan told me "I did transition work," with his many friends as he left his employment at his hospital. Nathan's connections knew him to be a person of integrity, caring, and experience. Some of his colleagues supported him with coaching opportunities and the chance to do limited term jobs as he went through his transition.

The leaders with whom I spoke agreed with Nathan: Their connections helped them in many ways as they journeyed through the darkness of the transition, through the storm, and beyond as they continued to create their success. The leadership journey is not a solo act; emerging leaders learn that their relationships help to define their impact.

MOVE PEOPLE WITH IDEAS

One of the leaders I interviewed wrote a book while working in her job. Having written a book, she contributed her work to the library at the company where she worked. Her book was constantly checked out. Her colleagues persistently asked her about her book, the culmination of her insight in that workplace. My friend added another copy to the resource room. Her experience, crystallized into a written volume, helped many others with their challenges on the job.

Ideas move people. Ideas generate creative dissatisfaction, an irritation to the soul that pushes people into action. Some people hear the call of a great idea, and bring others with them. A great idea creates an imperative. This force, moving people, can assemble many into a common purpose. A leader can use insight, oratory, and emotional intelligence to bind uncollected colleagues into a unified force.

Ted was asked to collaborate on a book with a best-selling author. Ted told me, "I want to change lives and serve a positive purpose." When he discovered that his work served other people, he applied this idea to his writing projects, and worked harder than ever to create new success in his life.

BE RESPONSIBLE FOR YOUR PEOPLE

Leaders are responsible to their people. The leader who cares, in a responsible way, feels a compassionate connection with all followers. Good leaders want their colleagues to grow and learn from challenging work. Responsibility is a theme of compassionate action for any sincere leader.

One career-changer told me how moved she was by the commitment her team offered to her in her new job. Her colleagues offered their pledges to stick with her during all coming work challenges. My friend was inspired by the intensity of connection offered to her. Turning inward, she had more insight about how other people worked. Effective leaders choose to practice responsible concern for their followers and the performance of the company.

Emerging leaders should pay attention to the motivations of their followers. People are all different; a motivating reason that moves one person may show us how to connect with the hearts of other connections. A resonating spirit is shared in a circle of friends; the leader should listen and observe with patience.

PROMOTE YOUR PEOPLE

Non-leaders often see the leader on top of their business or organization. Robert Townsend, in *Up the Organization*, wrote, "Leaders do dog work when necessary." Dr. Jack King, founder of the North Fork Center for Servant Leadership, said about potential leaders, "If you are not behind and beneath them, edifying, uplifting, helping them achieve their dreams and their vision, you're not leading." A true leader doesn't focus on the hierarchy.

It's just not important. To the leader, what is important is the quality of the relationship with the people connected to him. Leaders are interested in ensuring that the followers move forward–which is opposite to sustaining a hierarchy!

Eden was one of the experienced corporate leaders I talked to in preparing this book. Her work in aerospace led her to become an expert on business planning and supply chain problems. Eventually, she earned awards for her expertise and compassion in working with people. Eden told me that her growth as a leader came as she established meaningful relationships.

A number of the leaders in transition told me that they changed as they worked with people. The challenge of creating results through other persons, while promoting inspiration and inner-directed effort, often means that the leader must get out of the way of other people's effort. Kade made a work transition from a master hair stylist to opening a new franchise with schools and parents as customers. He found that he had to change how he approached people.

One manager in a state office of a federal agency talked to me during the period where she was promoted to replace her retiring manager. Hired as the agency manager on a provisional basis, she survived a trial period and the national office head confirmed her in the senior role for her state. Despite appearances and the logic of the organizational chart, this manager told me that she had to rely on a willing connection with her former peers in order to get the best results with the people she knew well as peers.

Influence, not command, is important to effective leaders. The power of the hierarchy is limited in its impact.

GET ENERGIZED BY PEOPLE

Our connections can energize us. Leaders discover that connected people are a power source for implementing action. With people by our side, we find methods to reach our goals easier, and the experience can be exhilarating.

A leader can build energy by offering enthusiasm and persistence toward worthwhile purpose. Other people respond to the style of a leader. Determination and a positive nature can be contagious.

A leader can build energy by offering enthusiasm and persistence toward worthwhile purpose. Other people respond to the style of a leader. "Excitement, learning, and meeting new people; gaining exposure to new people I never would have met stimulates me. It's exciting to learn from them." A small business owner, prominent in her community, shared this insight with me.

"The quality of the people you work with is really important." In *Phoenix Focus,* July 2010

Simply being surrounded by other people, sharing a diversity of experience and perspective, can energize people. The leader connects a team with common interests. The vision and organizing purpose attracts the effort of a quality team. People have different strengths and life perspectives that stimulate the thinking and activity of others.

One career-changer told me how important a community job network was to him as he worked through his transition period. I have also felt this energizing influence from a job support group; when others assemble with a common purpose, bringing ideas and leads to each other, the spirit is lifted during a period of doubt and uncertainty. The common purpose, the aligning of hearts and minds, and this level of connection add energy to the members of a group.

Much of the twenty-first century experience separates us. As good as television, movies, social media, and other forms of entertainment have become, these channels offer us diversion, yet the connections are often superficial. One Florida-based technology leader told me, "Now we live in a time of virtual offices."

I believe that many people search for meaningful connection, yet will not go through the effort to create a substantial bond. Eddie, a scholar and counselor in Louisiana, said, "We need to offer greater connection and touchability with people."

Other people simply don't feel that meaningful work is part of their lives, don't know how to choose substance over fashion. Leaders help to join people in a meaningful way.

BE PASSIONATE ABOUT THE PEOPLE AROUND YOU

"In the long run, people skills are more important than technical skills." – A project director in health care construction.

Great decision-makers know that people skills are essential.

In a new career, enter with a technical skill. Hiring managers think about the technical aspects of the jobs. The managers imagine blueprints and software, and skilled people who don't need sophisticated training to fill a specific set of functions. I rarely see job listings that call for workers with great people skills. Many businesses are content to hire highly skilled technicians. Leadership requires much more. Advanced people skills are learned through life lessons and varieties of work experience.

Demonstrate competence. If you are new to a workplace, be sensitive to the human relations issues as well. "People don't care how much you know–until they know how much you care," said John C. Maxwell. People might only discuss technical issues, however, you may be judged without an issue ever surfacing! Your skill in handling people issues will grow in importance as you establish yourself in your career. Others may bluster and shout about minor points. Grow in influence by employing people skills. Treat other people's issues with due consideration. Knowledge of the emotional content in the workplace can help one create alliances, building influence. People skills allow one to leverage other people's talents for a common purpose.

> **LESSONS FOR LEADERS**
> *Expand your circle of influence. Do this intentionally.*

Chapter 9 - Energy

Are you in transition? You may experience uncertainty, false starts, expenses, and role confusion. The person who changes careers has little promise that the destination will be a better place than that which was departed. Nevertheless, the career transitioner senses that something better lies ahead. The person who becomes a leader after a career transition offers personal assurances that the way ahead is worth exploring.

Career-changers and leaders demonstrate high levels of energy in order to reach their goals, and to persuade others to follow. Energy must be available at moments of crisis to assure others that the route is secure, and energy must be plentiful during less stressful moments in order to sustain the morale of connections and followers. Although high energy is inspiring, leaders and those in transition are mortal. High energy often leads to periods of energy troughs. The person in transition is not a continuous high-energy machine. We expect to see some downtime in all people.

> **DR. STEVE'S TIPS FOR LEADERS**
>
> Build your energy through these leadership practices:
>
> Find your purpose.
>
> Share and receive energy from other people.
>
> Get energized by new experiences.
>
> Enjoy the freedom to make your own choices.
>
> Get energized by learning.

In this chapter, emerging leaders talk about their energy levels as they created their new careers. Some people, like Karl, are serial entrepreneurs. When they discover a mission worthy of their life, they dedicate themselves to a sustained purpose. Finding one's purpose, according to the emerging leaders I talked with, results in additional personal energy. Leaders interact with other people, and this builds their energy level. Starting work with a new experience is energizing for many leaders. Leaders also experienced an energy lift through career freedom and through learning.

"Our energy is in proportion to the resistance it meets," according to William Hazlitt. Career-changers and leaders face certain challenge and resistance as they approach their goals; somehow their energy level rises to meet the needs of the situation. How many of us would start on a major life quest if we knew what we would face? Leaders and people in transition are notable because they acted and found the energy resources as they went along. Perhaps that is a reward for the brave soul: sufficient energy to face the challenge.

Denis Waitley tells us that the act of setting a goal itself provides the energy one needs: "Goals provide the energy source that powers our lives. One of the best ways we can get the most from the energy we have is to focus it. That is what goals can do for us; concentrate our energy." Leaders and people going through career transition typically do set goals, focus on their objectives, and marshal their energy.

Leaders are ready to move to action. According to James Thomas, "To be a great leader and so always master of the situation, one must of necessity have been a great thinker in action. An eagle was never yet hatched from a goose's egg." Action shows others the willingness to commit resources, personal energy, and one's reputation to one's vision. A good leader helps others take action. Energy sparks the action, with a vision-inspired purpose defining the course of action.

Kouzes and Posner, in *The Leadership Challenge* (2002), tell us that it is important for the leader to balance vision and action for the benefit of followers. Actions are best understood as a series of incremental steps, as smooth and continuous as possible. However, followers will want to know the big purpose. The leader helps to sustain energy for forward momentum by alternating between the big picture and the immediate next step. Followers with this understanding can generate energy because their work is purposeful. "Small wins breed success and propel us down the path" (p. 213).

In addition, leaders engage followers by demonstrating "enthusiasm, determination, and a desire to make something happen" (Kouzes & Posner, 2002, p. 178). The spirit of the leader's vision is conveyed through intense desire to move forward. Energy becomes part of the transformational vitality conveyed by a leader.

Leaders are needed to initiate action, encourage others to keep going, and to find the energetic resources to maintain a forward motion when spirits decline. Some have called this ability the power of leadership.

> Power is the basic energy needed to initiate and sustain action or, to put it another way, the capacity to translate intention into reality and sustain it. Leadership is the wise use of this power: Transformative leadership (Bennis & Nanus, 1985, p. 17).

Some leaders hold this power in restraint, bringing out their energy occasionally when needed to stimulate action. Other people perpetually simmer with energetic action and peppy behaviors. Bennis and Nanus note that leaders use power wisely, perhaps only applying the minimum force needed to spark needed action.

One concern of a leader is the development of other leaders. When a leader overuses energy and power, others may withdraw their actions. Wise leaders understand that their actions are best applied with restraint. Transformational leaders consider that when they apply too much energy and power, others might not learn to use their leadership skills. Leaders are aware that they are not working alone; they find the means to encourage others to use their nascent leadership skills. Sometimes, a great leader must encourage another to go forward, to show their proficiency and energetic action.

Energy gets people moving, and inspires confidence in the mission. Leaders apply energy skillfully, working with others in accord to create a stronger connection among followers to achieve goals. According to the career changers I interviewed, the skillful use of energy is an important quality in becoming a leader.

A SERIAL ENTREPRENEUR FINDS A MISSION

Some people recreate themselves regularly. Karl is such a person. Before his current mission, Karl held a number of jobs, opened several businesses, and ultimately sought work that brought meaning to his life. Karl told me, "I was always used to making money. I was never used to making a spiritual difference." What energized Karl was the chance to become a servant leader, work with a non-profit organization, and help hundreds of families and individuals in the North Phoenix area. He organized volunteers, served on the board of directors of a religious organization, and managed a 16-acre property with multiple buildings. He did not need this job financially, but he felt called to be part of this mission.

Most of us would not predict that a former cop would make such a career turn. After leaving police work, Karl became a radio disc jockey in Southern California. Later, he tried to find work without having a college diploma, and decided that it was important to pursue a higher education. Karl completed his MBA and opened a business. He was successful in his business, sold it, and started another. He became a specialist in financial services, and established a network of financial connections. Karl told me, "I've always been high energy." He started three businesses, and decided to retire.

Karl told me that he felt a spiritual calling to seek his current work. "I wasn't looking for another job, but after praying, I heard about this job opening. I felt it was meant for me, that God wanted me to apply for the job and start work." Shortly after submitting his application, he became the executive director of a non-profit organization. Does he have energy? "I'm working 60 hours per week now," Karl told me.

When we spoke, Karl told me about the great joy that he felt doing his work. He explained that he never is tired, but he does have to balance his personal needs with his commitment to the organization. He contributes sweat labor, inspires others to work hard as volunteers, and helps to write the strategic plan. He feels uniquely qualified in all areas to work in this way. Whenever I see Karl at his workplace, he is always busy, racing to take care of varied business and property needs. I have no doubt that Karl's joy is real, that he feels continuously energized about his chance to do meaningful work.

I recognize in Karl a man who has found important fulfillment in the work that he performs. He is not there working for the money; he works because of the energy return he gets from his work. He is recognized as a substantial contributor and servant leader in his non-profit community.

FIND YOUR PURPOSE

As Karl has demonstrated with his career, when one works with a special purpose in life, one has ample reserves of energy. Karl showed me that he is passionate about giving abundantly to his work; he believes in it. His heart moves him forward. Others have also found that working on a noble purpose provides one the energy to work hard.

Karl simply told me, "This is a great joy." His labors now match his dreams; Karl integrated the values in his life with his work, by helping others to make the world a better place. His heart and mind have found alignment with his spirit, and the nature of work lifts him.

Are you on purpose with your personal vision in life? Edwina told me that she realized her purpose was to help small and medium size businesses succeed. "I got a lot of energy from the realization that this is the work I was meant to do." Edwina found a deep source of energy from this effort; "I combine passion with an opportunity to have an impact." As I spoke with her, she told me about how she applied her skills to her work. She made new choices, and acted on what she learned. She volunteered with a job board. She described her practical work as highly spiritual, and realized that helping people lifted her energy.

"I am re-careering to an avocation I have dreamed of for years. Once again, I am full of energy, excitement, anticipation. AND, having made changes before, I am prepared for the work to reach and fulfill my dreams," wrote one the leaders I interviewed. With each significant change, she was able to adjust the work of life to bring her closer to her inner rhythm.

Hank moved from a secure job as head of a U.S. national business, a brand well-known to consumers, and assumed the uncertain work of a consultant. He was fortunate to find job assignments soon after losing his job. "My first assignment was a big boost. It got my heart pumping," Hank told me. He told me of the great satisfaction that he felt sharing the lessons of his earlier business career with a new network of business leaders. He realized that he had the potential and skills within him, and he wished he had started long before. "I would have been ready ten years earlier, if I had gotten started then."

SHARE AND RECEIVE ENERGY FROM OTHER PEOPLE

Many of the leaders in transition I interviewed were energized by working with other people. Other people offer us fresh perspective, the challenge of expanding our influence, and the opportunity to do good work in an expanded circle. Emerging leaders are often team leaders,e called on to share our approach and insight with others. Leadership does not do its best work as a solo effort; in fact, it is hard to imagine what leadership could possibly mean disconnected from others.

Yuriko made this point to me. I visited her in a business office that she has operated for over twenty years. "Excitement, learning and meeting new people, gaining exposure to new people I never would have met stimulates me. It's exciting to learn from them," she said. Yuriko works in both business and government, as an elected city council member. Her office bubbled with energy as she effectively balanced her time and her staff, and keeps a dedicated lap top computer for each realm of her work. Somehow, she kept the division of her attention separate and organized.

"My step has a bounce that was not there before," Wade wrote about his new role for a manager in a financial services group. "I became passionate about protecting my team and leading by example. I felt the sense of urgency to be in the trenches with my team to achieve my goal." As a leader for a business with definite goals, managers feel a deep connection to lead their people forward, to share successes. Wade made sure that he was close to the action, and that his people could see him visibly engaged with his goals. His energy surged as he shared the challenge with his team.

Why do other people energize us? Many people are extraverted, and draw their energy from a connection to others. It is natural for some people to be energized from this connection. Yet it is also true for introverts, as I see myself, to find energy when we work toward a common goal with other people who share certain values and concepts with us. When I work with others to create something new, on deadline, I can feel my excitement climb. I believe that this kind of connection challenges us to work a little harder, to be seen well by other people, and to create an outcome that will serve everyone well.

When leaders share a meaningful purpose with their followers, they may feel stimulated and quicken their pace. We interpret this experience as extra energy. A good connection with people working with us usually lifts our energy.

One of the leaders in transition that I interviewed took a dissenting view. Karen runs a statewide organization, and is a psychologist by training. She now has many psychologists and counselors reporting to her. Karen told me "Being a director is lonely." For some leaders, the challenge of the work may isolate a person, and reduce energy, as Karen has discovered. I hope that Karen discovers her resilient source of personal power!

GET ENERGIZED BY NEW EXPERIENCES

Think of vacation. Recall an accomplishment that you've worked at, now recognized by your colleagues. Test drive a new car that makes your heart leap, or simply drive a new route home. A new perspective can stimulate us. Take time regularly to try things out a new way. New experiences energize us.

Our work and our careers are an important part of our focus. When we anticipate positive change, we expect an energy lift. When we work toward our dreams, our body and spirit supply us with the energy that we need to get there.

Many people fear change. However, leaders specialize in the business of change. If a change was started by a person (rather than natural forces or business conditions), it was likely a leader that produced the change. While some changes can instill fear, a career-changer intentionally seeks change. Making it happen lifts the spirit.

When I was struggling to get my dissertation approved, I found myself ruminating and discouraged over the challenges I faced. One friend recommended to me "drive home using a different route." Simply experiencing a new route for a drive home can force our minds into thinking in a new way, and this can stimulate further creative response. Small changes can have a big impact on our system. Emerging leaders find this energizing effect all the time.

Eric made a transition from pastoral care to a writer, changes which followed a series of other career changes. He told me, "This last change has been enormous. The energy boost can be massive." He also added that leaders consume a great deal of energy as well; "A leader can require a great physical demand on his system." He emphasizes that the energy required to pursue personal change can be substantial, even physically draining.

Changes also lift us. One of my anonymous responders told me, "I felt excitement and a great deal of motivation to make changes in my career. As a result, I have had a very interesting, diverse, and rewarding life." Remembering this effect can be a powerful reason for launching our career change or business start!

Isaac had a lucrative career creating software solutions for financial traders on Wall Street. After making a change training business and organizational leaders, he felt charged: "My new work lit my fire, and connected me with my purpose. Now, the energy never dies down. I don't notice the time going by because I love doing what I do." Isaac is completely engaged about the possibilities he sees working with people in his field.

ENJOY THE FREEDOM OF MAKING YOUR OWN CHOICES

Career change can be inspired by a love of freedom, among other things. Job changers and business builder may have an internal dialogue around the subject of freedom: "I want to do my own thing." "I don't want to answer to a boss anymore," and "I would like to see how well I do on my own." The men and women I interviewed told me that this search for freedom charged them with extra energy.

When we get on the right track, other people can see our positive change. Neil contacted me through the Internet, and told me about a career change that he had worked on for several years. "People told me I seem to have a lot more energy and enthusiasm," wrote Neil.

We looked at Nathan's career change in Chapter 8. He left a structured job in a hospital and became an instructor, writer, and career advocate for nurses. He experienced the freedom that many entrepreneurs seek. "Now, my big dilemma is, which of the fun things should I do today?" Nathan disciplined himself to focus on his important tasks with his new role; without a boss, he chooses how to spend his working hours. Nevertheless, work remains fun for Nathan, and he loves his new freedom. "I get to focus on the things that energize me," he said.

Trent owned a successful advertising agency in the Midwest, and became a writer after a business reversal. Although he was used to being the boss and business owner in his previous career, he is ecstatic now about his current lifestyle choice. Trent told me, "I have incredible freedom in working from home." He affirmed the lift of energy he felt.

Career changers and emerging leaders do get to select some aspects of their new life. Freedom is important to many people, and when they can be productive while working on meaningful goals, they can feel energized. Freedom is a refreshing lift for a person who is used to working on other people's schedules. Following one's own passion can liberate energy to get more done.

GET ENERGIZED BY LEARNING

Learning takes more work than simply reacting. Doing the same old thing, acting as we always did it before, is often a brainless choice. However, for people working on career change, learning is essential. Career change is about learning and performing effectively in new roles. Most of us need to be conscious about the new choices we make in a career change.

Some people are excited to work with new ideas. When a person is working to change a system, the context of work itself, people must consider new ideas that work in the new relationship between workers and the employer.

Transformational leaders create game-changing conditions, starting with ideas, and engaging with other people. Intellectual stimulation happens when a real leader shares ideas with interested followers. Leaders and followers learn more about the world they create together, and this mental activity can energize people to action.

Yuriko entered politics after building a financial services business. She was stimulated through working with people, and with the new career role, she found that she had to learn in order to move ahead. She listed "learning" as one of the factors that brought her energy. Learning helped her master the context of politics.

Why does learning energize us?

Perhaps the career changer is able to apply new insights to the transition, to past jobs and future opportunities. A new framework of thinking shows us what we have experienced before with an expanded ability be effective. A career-changer and emerging leader may feel a "pull" toward a better future, and learning shows the person in transition how to take steps forward. New realizations bring hope, and the way out of transition becomes clearer. Seeing possibility may charge one with the energy needed to proceed forward.

Additionally, leaders share their ideas with followers. Learning becomes part of the community of knowledge, and helps all players become more effective. A synergy effect between followers and leaders helps everyone utilize better knowledge and become energized together.

ENERGY SUPPORTS CAREER BREAKTHROUGH

Leaders and career changers expect to create breakthroughs in their work. Energy is required to get there; energy also inspires others. We know that people are not always "on" with their energy; our bodies need time to recover. High-energy people should protect their health and continued vitality by finding moments to restore and reflect.

Find your energy source, and protect it. Your health and positive attitude are channels for transmitting the gift of vision that you carry from the well of wisdom. Just as a leader sets goals and connects with people, an effective leader must look at the energy balance in life and work necessary to achieve objectives.

Leaders are capable of taking action when the conditions are right. More than the readiness for action, leaders help followers prepare to act. Leaders encourage followers to engage with the same vision that sparks the leader's energy. Knowledge of the leader's vision-inspired purpose can become a source of reliable energy for followers, and help to sustain long-term action.

Followers can generate energy themselves once they have connected with an authentic leader's vision. Energy and intellectual stimulation contain a transformational vitality. Leaders help colleagues catch the flame.

Leaders build other leaders. In Buddhism, knowledge is a transmission of wisdom from teacher to student, very personal and deeply transformational. Leaders in our world of work and service also transmit a powerful *dharma* to followers, and part of this transmission is energy. Energy carries the vitality of the message.

A leader may be too involved, however, and stifle the expression of a follower. As in the condition of a parent who always picks up after a child, the child becomes dependent on the parent's actions, assuming it will always be there. A leader remembers that followers must deliver their own energy, develop their own capacity for action, and test their own wisdom as leaders.

Applied with wisdom, a leader will regulate the amount of energy applied at work. A leader understands that his or her energy changes the conditions of connection and the impact of action. When a leader overuses energy, others may hold their power in abeyance. A leader regularly assesses and anticipates that others will look to the leader before acting. Leaders apply energy skillfully.

Karl showed me that finding one's mission and purpose in work can be transformational. Karl exemplified for me the person who never has to work again in his life, because he is at home (spiritually) even as he's working. I wish this same life-changing experience for all of us. We would surely enjoy working with people in this condition so much that our own transformation comes easier. As we claim our purpose in our labor, our work rewards us with abundant vitality. Would you agree that it is worth changing one's career to earn this gift of life?

> **LESSONS FOR LEADERS**
> *Leaders need high levels of energy. Protect and nurture your sources of energy.*
>
> *You won't need peak levels of energy all the time. Nevertheless, find the resilience that comes from restoring your energy so it is available to you.*

Chapter 10 - Leaders Inspire Learning

Leaders are great learners.

Our world changes even as we pursue our goals. Learning is an imperative for this complicated world. The successful leaders in transition pay attention to lessons from their changing world, and share ideas with their followers. Great leaders convert painful experience into career lessons, and share them generously.

Change is distressful. When many things change at one time, it can feel like a "storm," and I have come to see the turbulence surrounding an emerging leader as just that – a storm. In the path of a tornado, many things change. Learning by a leader is one way that people become stronger, and face the tumult of rapid changes.

Learning is an essential part of life and growth. It is a responsible posture for facing change. Career-changers and emerging leaders learn, and help others to learn, during their transition. Learning is a catalyst for personal change. Learning is usually a conscious, consensual process, though sometimes lessons arrive for us that we have not planned.

> **DR. STEVE'S TIPS FOR LEADERS**
>
> The work must be learned.
>
> Have an open attitude toward learning the lessons of transition.
>
> Learn about people.
>
> Help others learn.
>
> Be adaptive.

In changing careers, people often learn about their new work. New work requires understanding new technology, expanding relationships with new people, developing a vocabulary to match the job, and learning how to share information about what they are doing. None of these skills comes automatically; one must apply oneself and add new job competencies. Practical lessons about the nature of our work will change frequently as technology and our environment change, too.

Frequently, people learn about their own lives. In graduate management school, we called these the "soft skills" because life learning is difficult to quantify. In the midst of change, emerging leaders may find that they are unintentionally enrolled in a specialized course of learning about life and the way of work. Internal learning (I like this term better than "soft skills") may affect everything we do, as well as the practical, "hard" learning that follows new job and skill training.

We all have emotional experiences, and as we grow older, we learn about what our emotions mean for us. Leaders learn about their emotions just as they learn about the nature of work. Our emotional experience often allows us to develop self-confidence and the courage to take bold steps. Leaders are aware that learning is continuous. Over the course of our working lives, we should never stop learning.

"I am learning all the time. The tombstone will be my diploma" said Eartha Kitt. Leaders are often at the cutting edge of change. A disciplined attitude toward learning helps one adapt to the new experiences. Even when a leader or career-changer fails, one can benefit from the experience by squeezing a lesson out of the pain. Successful people have faced many failures –everything short of dying.

Learning is much more than being a student. Anyone can enroll in a history course. A class or a lesson directs our thinking. If I am going through a career change, then I should be ready to learn almost anything. Learning expands a person's ability to act effectively.

We always have the opportunity to identify nuances in our work, make connections between systems, and perceive the underlying structure. The learner may not have a teacher other than raw circumstance. "I am always ready to learn although I do not always like being taught," said Winston Churchill. Learning is an act of interpretation.

What is a career-changer ready to learn? The time of transition is an excellent time to discard old lessons that are no longer relevant. The storm of career change may force one to adopt new rules of life. The previous cycle of lessons adopted from work may not help. Old lessons may actually impede our progress. Antisthenes, a student of Socrates, observed, "The most useful piece of learning for the uses of life is to unlearn what is untrue." Critical thinking applied to old lessons may help us review extend what we know. The period of transition is useful partly to rebuild a sturdy new structure of knowledge, fit to support our future challenges.

The person in transition discards old lessons. A competitive business culture will expect its sales stars to act differently than a thoughtful project manager for an engineering firm. When the rules for success change in one's work, the truth we understand may change as well. "It is not hard to learn more. What is hard is to unlearn when you discover yourself wrong" said author Martin Fischer. Only with the mastery of multiple contexts in different work cultures–organizational realities differ!–can an experienced leader separate universal career truth from lessons useful in different jobs.

Dr. Marilee Adams argues that decision-makers face a clamor for results, and don't spend enough time questioning their circumstance. "Asking questions invigorates thinking, learning, action, and results," she wrote in *Action Learning and its Applications, Present and Future* (Boshyk and Dilworth, 2010). A person in transition will benefit from new questions to guide one forward. The regular practice of asking questions helps an emerging leader develop the posture of readiness to adapt to the changing world, and perceive the new order from the confusion of change.

Warren Bennis emphasizes that people learn about leadership "only experientially." The work of a leader places one into a dynamic situation with uncertain outcomes; hazards to one's own career and reputation are common. Leaders get hurt while they learn. The person in career transition braves many of these same challenges. With a mental framework of asking questions, viewing the world regularly with a fresh mind, and adapting frequently, the emerging leader has a chance to safely navigate to a calm harbor after the storm.

Learning can be a confusing state. To proceed into learning means that the emerging leader may need to discard old lessons, or even get hurt. The first steps of learning as a leader may be retrograde – the way forward is to move in reverse. Kouzes and Posner observed, "Consider the very shape of most learning curves: they invariably show performance going down before it goes up. Learning doesn't take place in the absence of mistakes. Leaders are simply great learners" (2002, p. 215). The entry into the world of transition feels scary and dangerous. The beginning of learning leaves one feeling vulnerable in a transition; we are less certain of our own knowledge.

KIRK: A JOURNEY FROM HAIR STYLIST TO SCIENCE EDUCATOR

I met Kirk at a business networking function. He appeared to be on stage every moment, living a dramatic part. Kirk owns a franchise business dedicated to sharing a passion for science with high school students. His programs are slightly weird, completely wacky, and a lot of fun. He fills his role with determined flair.

Back in 2002, Kirk had a completely different career role – he was a fashionable hair stylist, and a trainer of other stylists. He told me that he was a platform artist – hired by hair product manufacturers to teach and sell their product lines to other stylists. Kirk's energy expressed was contagious as we talked. "I built a state-of-the-art facility on High Street," he said.

The building owner for his major studio went into bankruptcy. The hair products companies started playing politics with him. Big companies bought up smaller companies. Kirk's life entered the storm. He decided that it was time to enter a new business.

Kirk answered an advertisement to purchase a franchise. With his wife's support, Kirk looked into the business opportunity, and he liked what he saw. Even though he had never owned a business like his science tutoring company, Kirk adapted quickly. Instead of selling to fashion-conscious customers or hair stylists, he now prepared to sell his programs to schools and to families for special events.

He spent time shadowing another franchise owner, a successful businessman who mastered the relationships and context that Kirk had stepped into. After spending more than a week visiting a business in another state, learning how to make his business work, Kirk kept his mentor on speed dial, calling him regularly to check on the direction he was taking.

Kirk told me, "My learning curve is fast." Especially in dealing with his new customers, schools and their district leaders, decisions were made at a glacial pace. Kirk came to understand the process for making decisions, the importance of gatekeepers, and the challenge of keeping the attention of his prospective customers. "I changed how I approached people," said Kirk.

Most of Kirk's employees are contract teachers. He changed his working relationship from a "boss" to "lead teacher." "I came to see meetings as a great way to help them grow . . . I learned to say 'thank you' in business meetings."

Kirk also had to learn practical business tools like Quickbooks and the fundamentals of proposal-writing, invoicing, and accounts receivable. He adapted his business to conform to a business model established by a franchise authority. His new skills deepened his understanding of all kinds of business.

His metamorphosis has changed him from a flamboyant platform artist, selling to motivated hair stylists and independent business owners, into an educator and leader of teachers. He embodies the values of his new business fully, maintaining a dynamic stage presence to create and sell science education for kids.

Kirk has learned a great deal through his transition. He has learned to make money in a new kind of business. He has learned to treat his employees in a new way. He works with new kinds of customers. He has learned more about accounting, computing, and standard business practices. He launched this business with his wife, so he has learned to balance his personal life with his professional one on new terms. Throughout it all, Kirk is upbeat and contagiously interesting about his new career.

THE WORK MUST BE LEARNED

After a transition, one must learn the new job. Even (especially!) if one is the business owner, the work must be learned. There are details, regulations, accounting standards and new customer expectations. All of the details must be learned; the challenge is never trivial! Kirk not only had to learn about the new franchise business that he bought, he also had to learn accounting software in order to meet the program requirements.

One of the first challenges of an emerging leader and career changer is to learn the nature of the new rules. Once mastered, the rules will be shared–repeatedly–with followers. The education at work includes technical knowledge related to the work, developing relationships with the people who have expertise, and mastering the process of getting work done.

Katie made a transition from training employees in a foreign country, to working in customer service with a technology solutions company. "I did not know but I learned as a trainer I had to help other people learn. I rolled up my sleeves, and climbed under furniture to connect devices to a computer." Katie was not done learning at this point in her career; she later had another career transition and completed her MBA. *Once one becomes comfortable with lifelong learning, it may take you unexpected places.*

Kirk told me that it was important for him to be adaptive. He was used to selling to individual customers and small business owners; after his transition, he was selling to school districts and teachers. "They had little appreciation for the entrepreneur," Kirk said. The process, paperwork, and patience required to sell to a complex organization is typically much different from selling to individuals. The sales process requires a great deal of follow-up and record keeping needed to support a sale with a larger organization.

The technical details demand attention even after a leader makes a successful transition. Kimberly had a career in human resources that spanned several industries. "I was already a leader before I made my transition. I had to learn the technical skills after my career change." She emphasized to me that flexible leaders always have new learning in technical fields as they expand their scope of work.

HAVE AN OPEN ATTITUDE TOWARD LEARNING THE LESSONS OF TRANSITION

Although many transitioners have been successful in their past work, the storm changes everything. We spend our lives learning to be effective. Survival is a gift earned by those willing to learn. Leaders and career transitioners keep an open attitude toward learning. The world of transition is rarely predictable.

We learn about ourselves in times of transition. Nicole learned something important about herself, informing her about why she was dissatisfied with her earlier career. "I learned that I am an entrepreneur. When in the storm, the world of the transition, a person in transition may encounter a side to life that she hadn't known before. Difficult times present opportunities to see more of our inner world. In the previous section, we looked at Katie's career and education. She continues to learn throughout her life.

Another leader in transition, Beth, told me "I'm still going through it; the transformation never stops. We try to instill in our students a love of lifelong learning, which is an ongoing process." Beth came from a career in teaching and later opened a support program for women, and is working on a career as an author. Lifelong learning is an attitude that prepares one to shift when needed. Lifelong learning exhibits the open attitude toward personal education; giving one skills and mastery areas for unforeseen changes.

Edwina experienced three layoffs. "I found a way to maintain my positive attitude." Her positive approach helped her move to her next career.

Kimberly was mentioned earlier in this chapter. This woman embraces change with a strong positive attitude! As part of Kimberly's transition, "I left a position to earn my master's degree." Formal education both creates the credentials that others value, and offers new insight into one's own dynamics. Higher education, especially in the humanities and social sciences, teaches one to reflect about the values one uses at work. Higher education is one of the choices that leaders in transition have chosen to keep their attitude open toward learning.

LEARN ABOUT PEOPLE

One of my anonymous responders answered my question "Did you change as a leader?" with this thought:

> Loads! All to do with my development as a human being and refining my inner leadership. One of the most important [moments] was learning from an experience with someone who was 'inyerface' how my challenging could be construed as such and how I needed to refine how I did that. Other people told me I became 'softer,' i.e. more approachable.

Leaders are talented at working with people; every person may bring individual motivations and challenges to their work. Great leaders are students of workplace psychology. Some people challenge us, and block our progress. Other people hide their attacks, and "snipe" at us from protected positions. Leaders learn to safely proceed and expose attacks as they happen.

Leaders also learn how to see the hidden value in their people. Leaders help refine the natural talents of people in their circle of influence.

The Oxford English Dictionary has now added the expression "soft skills" as an official term. The OED definition is "interpersonal skills" and links the concept to emotional intelligence and social intelligence. Leaders are not the only people with soft skills, but leaders positively need to learn continuously in this area.

Eddie, mentioned in chapter eight, told me "The most fascinating thing about working with people is understanding their complexity and differences." He shared with me that through his transition from business into counseling, he felt doubts and uncertainty. Learning about people can provide the emotional life-jacket to help one succeed through periods of confusion. The neutral zone tests emerging leaders. Learning about people is a solid strategy for long term success.

HELP OTHERS LEARN

Leaders are often asked to be mentors for followers. People who have survived a career transition also help others go through similar experiences. The leaders in transition groups I interviewed have been advocates, coaches, and mentors for other people. Their lives have been broadened by the learning connection. Perspectives help us gain flexibility in changing conditions. The leader who helps others learn often expands his or her own insight.

Isaac, the Wall Street software specialist mentioned in Chapter 9, was profoundly changed by the lessons from his mentor. After his mentor passed away, Isaac carried on his teacher's message of compassion by teaching other leaders how to be authentic, and to face challenges while standing with values.

Saul described his career change to me, moving from being a "full-time professional musician and producer to computer geek." He now devotes his life to supporting a nonprofit think tank, and he represents the organization fully as a spokesperson that represents the integrity of the group. Saul told me, "from the president and others, I learned great core values, trust, and great customer relations." Values are one of the lessons that a leader must practice with authenticity, because people sense phonies.

Great leaders embody their values. Leaders don't just speak about the way of life they value – they live it. I've talked frequently with Saul, and have learned that his discussion of values is heartfelt and happy; he is passionate about helping people with his service. His passion is contagious!

Kirk modified his leadership style as he grew in his new business. When he holds meetings with employees, he uses the meetings to clarify the direction of the business. Meetings are an opportunity to share ideas, use team talent to solve problems, and educate others about the business.

Yuriko, the business professional and city council member introduced in Chapter 9, told me that helping others learn was stimulating. She became more effective, not only because she surrounded herself with informed followers, but also because she enjoys the process of sharing what she knows and has learned.

Helping others learn is an experience that changes people's lives! The modern experience of being a leader resembles acting like a teacher more than it does acting like a soldier. The leader who has internalized new life lessons has the chance to share his or her insight from the well of wisdom.

BE ADAPTIVE

Leaders navigate through change. Sometimes leaders cause the change; all too frequently, leaders protect and guide the organization through perilous times. The adaptive leader continually builds new strategies based on the changing world.

When I talked to Carl, the software entrepreneur introduced in Chapter 8, he emphasized the value of adaptability to me. Business leaders may only partly understand their markets when they launch their business. The test of an adaptive leader comes from a willingness to change the strategy based on the experience of reality. "I learned that you don't know your market until you get a product into the marketplace. . . . Learn from early market signals," said Carl as we spoke. The adaptive person is willing to adjust what has been learned before. New information may dramatically change how a business steers through the marketplace. The adaptive mind recognizes that what was learned before is valuable, and it may not be complete.

An adaptive person is willing to start with knowledge, take in more information, and change course as he moves forward. Kirk emphasized adaptability as we spoke. Even as he was learning about his new businesses, he had to learn about his customers and the way they worked. The practices that worked for him as a hair stylist, promoter, and sales person did not work when selling to school districts. Adaptability for Kirk meant that he reinvented his working style. He was mentally ready to learn while he moved forward. Flexibility in thinking is a great quality for leaders!

LEARNING IS A PERFORMANCE SKILL FOR LEADERS

John Kennedy wrote "leadership and learning are indispensable to each other."

Learning is a performance skill for leaders and career-changers. The work of change includes adapting strategies to new situations. Leaders and people in transition collect experiences, process them intellectually, and develop strategies for proceeding. Once success strategies have been built, our leaders in transition share that knowledge with others. Leadership learning is a process of disseminating experience with others, and also receiving knowledge from connected colleagues.

Learning is also a process of internal reflection, learning about the way that a manager relates to people, and building emotional intelligence about internal states. Leaders study both the business environment and their internal experience of the world. The leaders in transition I talked to saw both inner and outer reality, and learned from both.

Learning comes at a risk, as one can suffer and be hurt from the experience. Bennis spoke of the crucible experience that changes leaders forever. The transition from one career to another threatens economic pain, and the place between careers can lead one to disorientation: "Am I the person who worked on my last job? What kind of person am I becoming?" Our social roles often change during a transitional period.

Learn about the new work. Seek out people who have expertise, and connect with them. We spend part of our journey learning to be effective. The transition shows us that the old rules may no longer be important. Great leaders build a community of followers and smart sources who can interpret the way forward.

The challenge of learning while personal change is happening can leave a painful mark on one's psyche. Kirk showed us that with determination and an attitude to learn all one can, a person can learn about a radically new business context and come out ahead. When facing your transition, remember to learn the skills of the new environment, learn about yourself, and learn to appreciate the talents of the people in your connected circle. Build influence, and share what you have learned.

> **LESSONS FOR LEADERS**
>
> *If you are going to be a leader, you need to be in school, at least by your intention to learn. Be an advocate of learning, and model the value of learning for others.*

Chapter 11 - The Nature of Work

Work defines us. If a man sells real estate, he is known to be a person involved in the community. If one teaches kindergarten, then he or she will have long summer vacations, and the teacher is skilled at telling stories. A party planner is good at social relations, and must be organized as well as fun. The nature of work shapes a person's thoughts, directs our physical movements, and guides us toward future events.

Career-changers are in transition. They have arrived from one workplace experience, and possibly mastered it. If their change is successful, they will move to a new workplace with different tasks and expectations.

Our work challenges us to think about values and ideas. We may even be unaware how much our work defines our thoughts. Work often dominates our thoughts when we change careers. During the period of transition, one anticipates new issues, yet the reality of the new work may surprise and challenge thinking in ways unanticipated.

> **DR. STEVE'S TIPS FOR LEADERS**
> Go ahead, work hard.
> Make your work a priority.
> Live your values.
> Work with the politics and obstacles.
> Rise in the hierarchy.

Our work also shapes our social world. We have a relationship with a boss, customers, and with coworkers. We may do our work independently or in collaboration, and this working relationship will channel our thinking and behavior. We may laugh, listen, place cold calls, prepare a spreadsheet in silence, or discuss litigation with a team of legal specialists. Different manners of work guide every person's social behavior.

We work in different places. One man I know works in a hot laundry. Another trusted colleague runs an auto tune-up center under open garage docks, and constantly handles oil and grease. Many people work in restaurants, banks, and mines. Workplaces have rules that govern safety and health. Because of contact with the environment, chemicals, and radiation, we develop patterns of behavior that change us subtly but often profoundly.

The nature of our work influences the world we spend our time in, the people we talk to, and the ideas and values we think about. Work is a powerful field that guides our life while we are employed. A career change creates a profound shift in our life experience. Somehow, leaders become a master of their new world after a career change.

"By the work, one knows the workmen," said the French poet Jean de la Fontaine. The capability, and even the inner world of the laborer, is revealed by the quality of work produced. Leaders demonstrate their talent in the workplace, and often change the way work is conducted. A worker who achieves mastery over some part of the work, and can inspire others to do better work, is called a leader. A leader in the workplace delivers a substantial contribution to the process of work.

Work is partly a discipline of effort, yet many people find pleasure in their labors. A person who finds meaning in their work will often be satisfied with hard conditions, if he or she can make the world a little better. Creating joy in work is possible if the work supports deeply held values.

Leaders in Transition

> Never continue in a job you don't enjoy. If you're happy in what you're doing, you'll like yourself, you'll have inner peace. And if you have that, along with physical health, you will have had more success than you could possibly have imagined. ~ Johnny Carson

When a leader participates in the workplace, the reason for labor becomes important. Around a leader, people become inspired to find deep personal reasons to trade effort for the purchase of a purposeful life. Henry David Thoreau counseled, "Do not hire a man who does your work for money, but him who does it for love of it." A leader shows others why their work makes a difference.

A person's inner state radiates to others, and one can experience that state simply by spending time with the other person. If one works with joy, ease, and a positive outlook, then work is a valued part of one's life.

Warren Bennis (1999) has observed that most people fail to employ all their talents at work. According to Bennis, most people bring only about 5-10% of their skills to the workplace. If this skill gap were deeply understood, most organizations would be appalled at the poor use of resources.

Our work shapes our discipline, our character, and our skills. As we become more proficient in what we do, we have the chance to contribute more to our work. Some people – certainly not the leaders! – may be so detached from the purpose of their work, that they are willing to give less than they have within. The presence of leaders changes that dynamic. People get involved with their work around a leader of influence.

As leaders increase in their influence, they can inspire others to apply more of their talents, skills, and strengths. The presence of a leader among workers lifts the effectiveness of the organization. When workers understand the purpose of their work, they willingly bring their skills to the organization.

John Ruskin, the 19th century social critic, advises that people must have a sense of success in their work in order to find happiness. Workers inherently care about how well their organization is performing, when they see the workplace as a source of life happiness. People want to be effective, and to have others see them being effective. Leaders help people reach this state.

One of the essential practices of a good leader, according to Kouzes and Posner (2002), is to *challenge the process*. Work may be done in a certain way, and achieve predictable results. Managers rarely want to change a working system. A leader, on the other hand, may want to change the system. By asking, "what is possible?" the leader may intervene in the working situation. The leader may change the process by envisioning and selling an image of a better way of working. A leader may challenge a good status quo, and help engaged followers create a workplace that is more satisfying, inspires the soul, and achieves a lofty purpose.

Leaders participate in the nature of work, and they may change the way work is handled. Leaders review the way people work. They use their hearts and mind to find an optimal way to deliver results for the organization, and meet the needs of people at the same time.

A PATRIOT AND A COP

"The Army is a greatly controlled workplace," Dale told me. "When I went to work for a state government, I found it highly uncontrolled – even chaotic." Dale has worked for four different government agencies over the last twenty years. When he left college, he went to work for the Army as a paratrooper, and as a criminal investigator. Dale became a soldier, then a cop within the military system. Both of these descriptions defined Dale's work. "Coming up through the ranks was my first goal," said Dale. He has specialized in criminal investigations involving military personnel.

Over the years, Dale wore a number of different uniforms. He has worked for the Army, for the Air Force, and as a civilian, for state government and has fought the *War on Terror* as a special agent of the federal government. He has worked in the city and in the wilderness, always protecting the people of the United States and their armed forces.

"I had multiple voices that gave me structural obstacles. I was forced to play nice all the time," Dale told me. He is a creative innovator working in a rigid system, and the system has not always favored his approach, rewarding conformity over creativity.

At times, Dale has been challenged by his boss to stop exploring problems. The agency expects its officers to follow a disciplined style of work, and Dale has been told to stay within the box. As an innovator with an independent thinking style, he has been met by opposition with his higher-ups. Accordingly, I have changed a number of details about Dale's story in order to protect him. His boss has directly blocked at least one major project he has worked on, and he has spent thousands of hours recovering from this internal challenge. Nevertheless, Dale has held job security and has been able to advance his career.

Dale is a leader. He established an independent view for his agency. Dale stands up to authority and respectfully recommends change. Others have given him support behind the scenes and have modestly advanced Dale's approach.

Dale faced his boss down. He lived through a vigorous confrontation over work and values. Dale was forced to adapt, and he changed his outlook on work. He decided that his life was worth much more than his work allowed him to express. While still promoting his independent views, Dale has softened his approach and lets others be in control. He influences his agency as an independent voice but is not part of the governing coalition. After Dale's transforming encounter, his relationship with his work has changed.

Popular views show us a commanding general as a leader of a battalion, or someone similarly fierce. Dale is a different kind of leader. He transforms his workplace patiently but also steadily. I call Dale a "quiet leader" in his organization because he understands the nature of work, the expectations of his organization's culture, and remains dedicated toward improving the agency even if he isn't empowered with power and control. He is working to change a rigid system with a view of a better way to work.

GO AHEAD, WORK HARD

Work is often harder than we like. Leaders are pulled between doing "just enough" and the drive to take the organization to a better place. No matter how hard they work, career-changers may have difficulty reaching important milestones. A career change may require extraordinary effort in order to create a new normal state. In creating any business, most entrepreneurs face work that may never repay one's efforts.

Leaders have to be masters of the work in order to call for a better way.

> It does not seem to be true that work necessarily needs to be unpleasant. It may always have to be hard, or at least harder than doing nothing at all. But there is ample evidence that work can be enjoyable, and that indeed, it is often the most enjoyable part of life. ~ Mihaly Csikszentmihalyi

Career-changers may experience hard work, and find deep satisfaction from the fulfillment of the assignment. Karl, the entrepreneur discussed in Chapter 9 said "I can work 18 hours, even think about the idea when I am sleeping." The importance of work for an entrepreneur and a leader often approaches an obsession.

If you are changing your career, you will probably work long hours too. Carl was gripped by the importance of the change he was leading. The intensity of his focus gripped him so much that he started dreaming about changing his workplace.

Dale told me that as he experienced his most recent career change, "For the first time, work became a task." He did not enjoy his work after the boundaries were set by his boss. Nevertheless, his sense of integrity and connection with his mission challenged him to keep working with a high level of dedication. Leaders may not always like their work, even though inner purpose keeps them focused on the task.

"I'm serious about work. I'm a fanatical nut about getting results and perfection." Earl, a business technology leader, described his relationship with work with intense terms. He sets a high standard for the quality of his work. Many leaders are focused on the measurement and performance of the details at work. This critical intimacy with the nitty-gritty detail of work allows many leaders to share experiences and communicate with other workers at a knowing level. Followers know the hard-working leader "gets it." Leaders cannot fake this knowledge about the conditions in work.

Sam, a software expert and customer service maven, acknowledges the nature of work, and claims his attitude is part of his nature. "I've always identified with my work. I have a good work ethic."

MAKE WORK A PRIORITY

Leaders think their work is important. Not everyone shares this perspective; not everyone is a leader. Quitting time is an enjoyable moment for many laborers, yet leaders continue to think about the important work that lies ahead.

Hal made a change from a corporate executive, to a private consultant. He now enjoys working fewer hours, and works from home. He has happily made a trade-off that allows him increased leisure. He is also extremely proud that he has made a mental leap – he challenges his clients to take him seriously so that they won't waste his time. He has found that people listen to him, and take his advice, when he assertively challenges people. The fantastic paradox is that Hal works fewer hours, and continues to value his working time as vitally important to his self-image. He is excited that he can make a big impact with less effort.

Caitlin was excited to tell me that she changed careers, and she was able to create work that matched her strengths. Through creating a new business, Caitlin "found" her inner entrepreneur.

Describing the energy she gained in this career change, Caitlin said, "I found the right combination of matching my personality with my work." When the work matches the personality, people have fewer struggles and more joy in completing labor.

In Caitlin's discovery, she has moved beyond work politics she experienced in her previous career. Now, work is central to her life. Politics no longer keep her from enjoying work. "Politics translates into personalities. If you do not have a good personality/culture fit, it's probably not going to work out," Caitlin said. Her career change removed a barrier that prevented her from the full appreciation of work.

LIVE YOUR VALUES

Hours of labor, mind in focus, heart working in appreciation for people; our work advances certain values. More than most, leaders are aware that their work can change the world to be a better place, and conversely, through neglect or bad choices, lower the value of living. Many career-changers and emerging leaders understand that their values can be perceived through the choices made at work.

A salesman of software and equipment in technology, Kirk told me "Learn what you are good at; then decide how this contributes to the marketplace and community." In addition to his hours working, he dedicates some time to helping low-income kids learn job skills. "Be honest and truthful," he added as we spoke about his career.

Taylor was promoted to a mid-level management job in a federal agency. She spoke to me about the challenges of managing employees who were formerly her peers. She told me how important good communication became for her in her new role.

Tom changed his career from advertising to writing and other media. He admitted to me that he practiced "weak morals" in his first career, which "sometimes challenged my integrity." He is delighted now that his independent status as a writer allows him to be ethical in his work. "I won't take a ghost (writing) project unless I believe in it." Tom's sincere joy was obvious to perceive as I spoke with him.

People hold different values, yet it seems that leaders are clear and focused on their values. They actively uphold the values. Work creates many situations that reveal our moral nature. Leaders have had more opportunity than working followers to encounter the moral system that they follow. If you hear a person sincerely talking about their values, there is a good chance this person is a leader in his or her work and community.

WORK WITH POLITICS AND OBSTACLES

Few people enjoy politics–except perhaps for those who make a profession of it. In an earlier work, I talked to career-changers in education. Most teachers want to be a role model for students, and not lobby for resources. The way things are done sometimes depends on who you know, and what favors you are willing to do for others. Some organizations act more political than other workplaces do.

Politics and other obstacles are challenges for many people at work. In advancing an agenda, as leaders do, the emerging leader often confronts the political world of work, and the experience can be disillusioning to one's spirit.

Dale told me that he faced chaos and politics in moving through his career. "I learned how to work with the hierarchy and system," he said. In like manner, most leaders face the frustration of politics and growth through the challenge. It is part of organizational work. Leaders must learn, like Dale, to make a difference while surrounded by politics and obstacles.

Do you remember Katie, the young technology trainer introduced in Chapter 10? She told me that she faced the politics of her workplace; sometimes she had to adopt a professional exterior that just didn't feel natural to her. She adopted this style as a way of adapting to the culture and expectations of the workplace. In her own words, "The way I carry myself represents the company. I've redesigned how I look and how I carry myself."

In chapter 10, serial entrepreneur Carl talked about the challenges of changing his own company. He realized that he needed to be a force for change in his own company, even though the people he led did not want the situation to change. A natural momentum exists in most workplaces; people resist change when their own habits are involved. Carl's advice to leaders,: "You have to figure out a way to bridge that gap." Find a way to help people adjust to the changes you need to see happen.

Caitlin made her work a priority, but she did not enjoy the workplace politics. She discovered that she had to understand the personality needs of the people around her. In order to work with the politics of the situation, she found that she had to exert her influence in appropriate ways, taking into account her own style. When she changed careers, this work became easier for her, as she felt that she was now "in her element."

RISE IN THE HIERARCHY

Emerging leaders rise in their organizations. If a leader believes in the mission of the company, he or she will advance it. If the leader does not believe in the work or values, the leader may work to change it – and may be seen as a troublemaker. The career-changer in a corporate setting may have to be conscious of the politics and challenges around her, and make judicious changes at the right times. Too much change and the career-changer may plummet from a place of effectiveness. Too little effort and the impact doesn't matter. In order to rise in a complex organization, the emerging leader must have a sophisticated understanding of how the culture works.

Many emerging leaders work in a complex hierarchy. The climb up isn't enjoyable, and is not for everyone. Leaders with approved titles and authority can make change happen with greater ease than those who aren't titled. The nature of work requires many emerging leaders to become part of the system and seek organizational power. Seeking power can be a pragmatic approach to creating positive change.

WORK CAN BE A PLEASURE

> In order that people may be happy in their work, these three things are needed: They must be fit for it. They must not do too much of it. And they must have a sense of success in it. ~ John Ruskin

Work can be a challenging place. Career changers must navigate through a world of change, the old rules may no longer apply, and the challenges may come from unexpected regions. To be effective, emerging leaders must be ready to continually learn and adapt.

Our life experience is felt and expressed at work. A person comes to be defined by the work that he or she does. Career-changers seek to deal themselves into a new game, and leaders write themselves (and others) new rules for their work. Leaders are often game-changing.

Work directs our thoughts, and many people shape their ideas and values based on a world experienced at work. Leaders may not consciously make these choices. However, the outcome of a leader at work is that the values and standards at work may be redefined after a leader has intervened.

Career changers operate in a social world. Work restricts our free time, and connects us with new people. The career changer moves through one system, and into another. New rules apply. If the career changer emerges as a leader, the change in work may give the person an opportunity to rise in ways that were unavailable before the change.

Many leaders offer inspiration to others at work. They do this partly because they may have advanced skills, but certainly most leaders inspire because they advance certain values and show others how to change the way they work. Inspiration is one of the defining differences between a leader and a capable manager. A leader lifts the energy at work.

Is it farfetched to think that leaders inspire happier workplaces? If another person has found meaning in his or her work, then that person is more committed, more engaged with the work. A leader often is responsible for helping people to realize why their work makes a difference. People may contribute more passion to their labor.

Nevertheless, the career-changers in this study reported that they participated in hard work. Leaders have a reputation for working hard; they may lose sleep and set a difficult standard for others to match. Professionals do not master new fields by casual effort–especially not in a competitive economy. Mastery follows a period of hard work.

Leaders and career-changers seem to be obsessed with work. They both view work with dedicated focus, and even a serious intensity. An effective leader may become identified with the quality and outcomes of the work. Understanding the importance of a job in an organization is critical to the evolution of a leader. Leaders identify with their work, their mission, and their purpose. The care of their organization and its people is central to their attention.

A leader's work advances personal values. Many people are only vaguely aware of what they stand for. Leaders make many small and large decisions; the leader's values help one choose important actions. Leaders gain clarity about what they stand for as they advance their careers. Other people come to understand a leader's values through the legacy of decisions. Work is a place where leaders express values through action, and followers vividly understand the peril of hard decisions. Others may glimpse our moral nature when we lead an organization.

Leaders often face obstacles and politics at work. When people contribute to an effort, things often get complicated. People use their power and influence to do things their way. That's the nature of politics. People make the process of work more complicated than others would like. Career-changers often push their way forward in the face of obstacles they had not foreseen.

The organizational hierarchy is a formidable challenge mentioned by some of the career-changers in this study. Emerging leaders gain power as they rise in their organization's ladder. As one earns a better job title, a worker usually gains practical authority to accomplish his or her goals. An employee who moves closer to the executive's office usually has more connections and pragmatic power needed to accomplish major goals. The path up the hierarchy can be complex, with unexpected turns.

> **LESSONS FOR LEADERS**
>
> Even though you may work hard, take pleasure in the work you do.
>
> Don't think of work as a "necessary evil," think of work as a place to do good in the world. Most of your daily life will be spent at work — make it a positive time! Help others to work hard, and to enjoy their work too.
>
> Leaders inspire happier workplaces.

Chapter 12 - Goals and Results

Is it possible to think of leaders and managers, and not to think of goals? The work of a leader is not random; it is intentional. Leaders work to produce results. Career-changers also plan and work toward goals; career-changers are driven by an imperative to change their life in an important new direction. They feel urgency and determination. In my interviews with career changing leaders, I've found that leaders talk about goals regularly, in relation to their work and their lives.

Goals imply planning, effort, and the evaluation of a world made better by an engaged mind. Frequently, goals support other goals to achieve a larger purpose. A goal may be an intermediate event, and all efforts may be subsidiary to the organization's–or to one's personal mission. When a goal is accomplished, the leader and career-changer may have a reason to celebrate, even though the desired end-state has not been achieved. Progress is felt when successive goals are achieved, and a long-range vision appears closer with each milestone.

> **DR. STEVE'S TIPS FOR LEADERS**
>
> Know your long term goals.
>
> Solve problems.
>
> Get results for clients.
>
> Be focused, and work intentionally.
>
> Have financial goals.
>
> Put your goals in writing.

Career-changers become masters of their destinies by choosing their own goals. In doing this, they act like leaders. Leaders are always involved in goal setting, even though they may participate as an equal with others who set goals as a team effort.

Some people do not set goals. Some people don't measure their results. The person choosing a career change has made decisions about his or her future, and this may be a new experience. When career-changers intentionally direct their futures, they have adopted a mindset similar to a leader–a person who evaluates the direction of action and makes a commitment to proceed for an intended result.

It is possible that career-changers become better goal-setters while changing careers. The challenge of changing careers can open the door to leadership transformation through goal- setting and the determination to achieve meaningful results.

Self-mastery is an essential skill for the career-changer and emerging leader. A goal as high as Mount Everest can be achieved only given the discipline and knowledge of the climber. The first Everest climber, Edmond Hillary, wrote, "It is not the mountain we conquer, but ourselves." The achievement of a lofty goal depends on personal capability.

Goals are linked to time. We can measure our progress toward goals using time, or notice that our goals have become distant and less likely. "Every day that you spend drifting away from your goals is a waste not only of that day, but also of the additional day it takes to regain lost ground," said Ralph Marston. Leaders must not only take action, but they must also gauge their drift away from their purpose. Some drift may be expected, as our paths always encounter resistance. The passage of time may tell a person how expensive the drift is when compared to the outcome.

"Until we can manage time, we can manage nothing else." Peter Drucker, twentieth century's eminent voice on effective management, taught that people skill emerges from the skills we have over our own time. The achievement of goals requires mastery over one's own time and attention. The career-changer must treat his or her time as a scarce commodity, and use it judiciously.

Leaders and career-changers must know their goals, take action, and pause regularly to look at their progress. Warren Bennis has offered this paradoxical insight: "When you're going along, and everything is working well, you don't sit down and reflect. Which is exactly the moment you should do it" (1989, p. 116). Goals are important enough to the leader that evaluation of one's progress happens regularly. Even when the leader and team are advancing toward chosen milestones, leaders will review their progress.

Management scholars Kouzes and Posner (2002) emphasize that a leader communicates about the goals and direction of the organization. "There's nothing more demoralizing than a leader who can't clearly articulate why we're doing what we're doing" (Kouzes & Posner, 2002). The effective leader addresses the higher purpose of action, so that every member can discover the meaning of action. Knowing what action means to the enterprise, the member can then contribute to achievement. Leaders change the enthusiasm of the members of a team by invoking a high purpose. If a leader cannot connect followers' actions to this purpose, the result can be demoralizing.

Career-changers are deeply involved in the communication of goals. For the career changer, the most important career belief must be personal. If one's life and career are to change, speech and ideas will reflect conviction about the career-changer's goals and their outcomes. The career- changer must speak convincingly about his or her transition, and have a heart changed by the commitment to a new purpose. Career change reflects an internal transformation, and the words that we use reflect our values and relationship to our goals.

FROM CORPORATE CITIZEN TO ENTREPRENEUR

In Chapter 9, we briefly examined the energy of Edwina. Previously working as a corporate executive, she changed her career. Edwina's career soared high in the world of manufacturing and business logistics, and she was quite proud of a leadership award she earned: "I was nominated by my team. This meant a lot to me!" She now defines herself as a private business leader and coach for other executives. Edwina told me that she enjoys her life much more, and discovered that she works with high levels of energy.

Edwina was a focused leader throughout her career. Goals have been an essential part of her corporate work life. She worked in logistics, progressing through five sequential career steps over a 19-year career for the same aerospace and technology firm. Her career moved forward consistently; the horizon always expanded forward. She learned to operate as an original equipment manufacturer (OEM); she helped other businesses meet their goals through the resale of technology. Edwina once had 55 people reporting to her in the manufacture of aerospace technology. She has also worked as a buyer, and as a logistics specialist. Having succeeded in these roles, Edwina became a planner for the business.

Having achieved success as a manufacturing leader, she moved to the product aftermarket. She developed an extensive network of decision-makers in the aviation community. Edwina helped others achieve their business goals as a product collaborator. She established herself as a senior manager with important connections throughout the aerospace community.

Another multinational aviation firm purchased her company. Significantly, Edwina was now directed to help integrate the two companies. She helped both organizations communicate and integrate their goals. In addition, she installed a Six Sigma system for creating workplace quality. Much of her work now migrated toward establishing common measures and practices between the two former competitors. This work involved not only setting goals, but also the work of establishing a new culture in the midst of rapid change.

Her work had continuously been involved in goal setting. Edwina measured performance, collaborated with others, and promoted plan change between complex organizational systems. She developed a range of skills valuable for internal leadership as well as external relations. Apparently, this was not enough.

The multinational business laid Edwina off. She chose not to seek employment with part of her extended network of colleagues. After two decades of continuous growth and change, she now had to redefine herself. "I felt shackled in the corporate world," Edwina told me. "I had to do something I felt sincere about."

Our former corporate citizen engaged herself in a personal learning program. She joined a networking group, read deeply, and expanded her connections in the community. Edwina now worked for learning, reflection, and challenging herself to set goals and personal career decisions in new directions.

Edwina went through a transformation. Never abandoning the discipline and focused work ethic that she had established through her work in the manufacturing environment, she now saw herself as a teacher and mentor for other business leaders. "I made a decision to work with small and medium size business leaders. Once I clearly saw this new direction for me, I found a great deal of energy that helped me forward in creating my new career," Edwina said.

Edwina applied herself to the process of transformation with dedication. Yes, she faced periods of "panic" (her word), and still does, but she never regrets the new direction in her life. Did she change as a leader? Not really, she told me; she is still the same kind of leader. What has changed is the way she works. "I feel freedom and the flexibility of being a small business owner. And the rewards are amazing," Edwina told me with confidence.

Edwina's choice to transform the way she works is a reflection of her disciplined approach to handling goals and outcomes. She is friendly with her clients, and yet "all-business" in her demeanor. Her professional manner and enthusiastic adaptation of her work following a change is a positive reminder for all career-changers that major life adaptations can be successful and fulfilling.

KNOW YOUR LONG TERM GOALS

The career changers I talked to have worked with long-term goals. They keep a horizon measured in years, and understand that big results require a determined focus. A long term goal is closely related to one's purpose in life. Leaders bring us closer to our purpose.

"Talk to career-changers about their long-term goals." This was the advice given to me by Dale, the patriot and cop I profiled in Chapter 8. It is important for career-changers to know their personal objectives, and to develop the clarity that comes from a deep study of one's values and purpose. The long-term goal is therefore a constant for the person in career transition; it should be a bedrock of determination.

Sam launched a new career moving from work as a professional musician, well acquainted with headline acts on the East Coast. Sam's transition was an entry into the field of IT, which required learning new disciplines of work. For him, the effort at transition required a long-term commitment. He recently has been promoted to an information officer for IT and customer support professionals, speaking and writing as an advocate for people who support people with technology. His dedication to his long-term goal expanded his perspective on life, work, and career.

Yuriko, introduced in Chapter 6, made her transition into the world of city government politics. She spoke about long-term goals that she was able to accomplish for her city, a multi-million dollar sports building and contract with a university and sports team. As she has developed new areas of influence and works with new disciplines of work, she has put her attention increasingly to long-term projects. She values the successes that leave a legacy behind for her community. She is proud of what she has achieved with other civic leaders.

Tara was promoted to succeed her boss. I spoke to her during her period of transition, before her promotion had been made official. She told me that cultivating a vision and establishing several long-term goals would be important to her as she began her new career, a change from engineer to manager.

For career-changers and emerging leaders, the role of long-term goals are important for establishing a compass to direct daily efforts. The long-term goal reminds us that our work is cumulative, and planning is essential for big achievements. The leader is capable of moving people toward a remarkable destination, one that inspires others to go farther.

SOLVE PROBLEMS

Leaders leave the world a better place. Career-changers seek to improve their situation, and the situation for their customers and followers. Both leaders and career-changers may aim for a state of perfection, yet the world is a sticky place where problems can be complicated with new challenges regularly encountered. Leaders and people in career transition solve problems to gain momentum on the long-term goals.

Leaders change the context by solving fundamental problems. Earl, a business leader discussed in chapter 8, told me "I was fascinated by how companies succeed in spite of their actions! As a leader, I try to take the mistakes and remove them from my equation." Managers may persist with established systems in the face of change. It is an act of leadership to solve problems and help the organization thrive even while conditions have adapted to new world conditions.

Karen, an executive director for a nonprofit organization (mentioned in chapter 6) had been promoted after many years providing professional services. She saw many opportunities for improvement in her organization, and found that people supported her work. "I worked on getting results, and improved the processes. I gained a reputation for getting things done. " After several years of leading change, Karen has broad support in her agency. "I saw the system improve and thrive, and that has been very satisfying to me."

Isaac, mentioned earlier in chapter 6, solved client problems using technology. As he became a more experienced leader, he learned to solve problems in a collaborative manner. He did more than intervene – he paid attention to the way his clients worked, involving them in a discussion. Isaac solved problems using the talents of other people. His clients became part of their own solution process.

Goals and results are achieved after a dedicated worker applies thought and action to the problems. Leaders don't just solve problems, they solve the underlying problems that keep people from becoming most effective. Career-changers may encounter their own problems when transforming their circumstances; the successful transition will include solved problems. Transformation may follow when an intelligent leader changes the fundamentals in a situation. After a transformational problem has been solved, people work in new ways.

GET RESULTS FOR CLIENTS

A number of the leaders in my discussions told me that they produced results for their clients and customers. It isn't enough to simply work hard. Anyone might work hard without achieving results. Results indicate that a beneficial outcome was achieved. The results move one closer to a victory.

"I made sure that we had something beneficial that the client could pay for and/or recommend," said Kirk, who was introduced in Chapter 8. Kirk holds a strong sense of values about his work; it is important to his personal sense of justice that his work improves the life of clients. Kirk wanted his reputation for quality to precede him, based on the experience of value served to his clients.

In her public service organization, Karen told me how important it was to make a difference in people's lives. She felt fulfilled through this achievement. Originally working as a counselor for clients, now working as a leader of counselors, she had the opportunity to improve the lives of more people, although she saw less of her clients. Her direct clients now are the counselors, psychologists, and health professionals who work for her. She helps them become more effective. Among service providers, she has a rare appreciation that a leadership role also makes a difference for many people.

Leaders have Karen's capacity to learn a trade, and then learn how to help others become more effective. They extend their service to more people, helping many others get great results. Career-changers often move into new fields with a background that gives them extra potential to help clients. The direct client of a leader is the follower. When a leader like Karen helps others become more effective, the benefit of the service is extended widely.

Thomas made a transition from a lawyer to a professional mediator. He now helps his clients, often men and women involved with divorce, solve problems with less cost and frustration. Instead of using two lawyers to fight over a position, Thomas helps clients resolve issues with the perspective of law and justice. He knows how judges are likely to settle a case, and he helps reach a solution faster. He told me, "I've helped thousands of people, and kept them out of court."

BE FOCUSED. WORK INTENTIONALLY

The best goals are clear. They specify a precise target. When a career-changer can set her direction with focus, she will spend less effort in getting results. Focus helps to eliminate extra effort. Leaders benefit from intentionally choosing their targets and pursuing them with determination. The clear pursuit of a well-chosen goal can be inspiring to others.

One of my anonymous responders told me that emerging leaders should "Develop a concrete plan and stick to it. Ignore the negative, but pay attention to honest, positive critique and guidance. Seek a mentor in the chosen field. Keep it simple." This suggestion emphasizes planning and learning. The career-changer's plan anticipates the future, and learning helps one respond effectively to new circumstances.

Edwina told me that leaders use intentional effort to make a big result. "I decided to work with the goals I am aligned by. I decided to live intentionally." Intentional living means making up one's own mind about the future, and pursuing one's goals with determination.

Creating a focused approach suggests that time and energy are not wasted on side projects. The successful person applies the ability to focus one's mind, and make choices. Once the focus is established, emerging leaders should take action swiftly. All thoughts of hesitation and doubt should be minimal. Clarity of mind frees one to act without impediment.

HAVE FINANCIAL GOALS

Several of the career-changers emphasized financial goals as an important part of their effort. The financial goal converts a good idea into a marketplace activity or another measured result with financial consequences. If the leader works for a nonprofit or government organization, the financial goal is equally valued, perhaps in the form of economic efficiency or effective service toward the clientele. Financial goals demonstrate that the leader and organization are working on a sustained economic reality. Money, costs, and all resources are important to an effective organization.

Carl, the software entrepreneur introduced in Chapter 5, told me that financial goals are very important for the motivation of the followers in a business. The entrepreneur may have settled on a milliondollar revenue goal, yet he keeps working to exceed that. His or her goal often extends outward, creating a bolder vision of what is possible. When his company first achieves the million dollar revenue goal, the employees in the business may be very excited – yet the business leader is already looking beyond, perhaps to the ten million dollar goal. An inspired leader keeps pushing the horizon outward.

The leader's goal continually pushes forward. The staff members of that business may not have their focus shifted in synchrony with the leader. The work of the business leader is to continually challenge followers to look further, and to share an expanding horizon.

Tom (see Chapter 8) told me that in the 1990s, his goal was to retire, and to have a lot of toys. He once had a boat, fancy cars, and expensive sports tickets for his friends and clients. He led a good life! Tom lamented that he took his focus off his business, and lost everything. He recalled sitting in a deserted advertising office with marked price tags on the furniture and equipment. Everything was sold that could be sold. Tom's lesson was that it wasn't enough to have goals for one's life, it was also important to have goals for his business – and to watch the store.

Financial goals should be set for the organization, just as we have goals for our personal life. The leader is a remarkable person who cares for the well-being of the business, agency, and followers, and enlists others into the care of those goals. The career-changer may become an emergent leader through adopting a servant attitude. The financial goals of the organization are fundamental to the sustained health of the mission. For engaged leaders, these goals are not just a job; they are a passion.

PUT YOUR GOALS IN WRITING

Tom continues to recommend that all leaders and career changers write down their goals. Although he went through a significant financial reversal, he made sure that all of his creditors were paid, even if the payment period took years. Tom felt it was important to have the inner integrity that follows from knowing all his financial promises were kept in the best way that he could achieve. Written goals helped Tom achieve this purpose.

Some advocates of the *law of attraction* argue that written goals make us more powerful, sending us powerful new energy that we can use to achieve our purpose. Some of the discussion of written goals sounds, frankly, magical. However, I have found that written goals crystallize my thinking, help me focus on my priorities, and make it easier for me to take advantage of new opportunities.

I don't like to depend on magical processes; however, I think there are mysteries to be learned. I think achievers can discover for themselves how positive intention and clear thinking can create more for a leader and a career-changer than inaction and dullness will. A positive intention seems to pave the way for further achievement. Written goals support this clarity and help a person move closer to his or her dreams.

Dale, the *war on terror* federal agent discussed in chapter 11, told me that he never doubted that his goals were right. In various government agencies, he felt an essential rightness about the direction he chose for his work. The clarity of his goals helped Dale persist in his efforts even while facing negativity from his superior officers.

Written goals create a firm measure of intention. Our minds may trick us after the fact; we thought our goal was X, but at the time set, it was really X+5. Most intelligent people can be regularly fooled by a mind that helps the person stay "right" no matter what happens. A written goal prevents a certain amount of "creep" away from the original target. Written goals keep us focused on what is important, and help to prevent a career-changer from changing direction without full consideration. The career-changer with a written goal has a solid target to direct his or her activities.

GOALS LEAD YOU TO VICTORY

Goals are the foundation of leadership action. Especially true for anyone working to change his or her career, the goal transfers a desire into something definite. A goal can be shared, measured, and can involve more than a single person. A goal moves one closer to positive action.

Goals are important for the career-changer, as the person in one career creates a highway through space, into an unknown valley where he or she has never gone before. Goals allow us to assess our forward momentum. Leaders frequently talk about the value of their goals as a mental activity that leads to important action.

Goals may be stacked together to create a major life accomplishment. The career-changer, like the leader, moves into unknown territory. The sequence of goals allows a person moving through change to know that the effort is purposeful. A purposeful sequence allows one to have the advantage of mind power applied to their actions.

I believe that when career-changers firmly commit to their goals, they become masters of their destinies. They have chosen to control the way they think, they have evaluated their choices, and they have selected a set of actions that increase the likelihood of learning and eventual success. The career-changer becomes a better leader simply by learning how goals help one achieve great things.

The quality of self-mastery helps anyone achieve important career goals. Eventually, one will encounter resistance in the pursuit of any important project. The ability to apply a disciplined effort at achieving goals means that resistance has met an opposing force for change! When the career-changer applies knowledge, determination, and the power of a network, the ability to move through resistance is increased.

Forward momentum is not the only factor that supports achievement. Career-changers should pause regularly to review their effort. In addition to deciding if the actions are the best choices for the situation, people in transition may want to look inward and assess their own motivation. Is the career-changer driven out of selfish reasons alone? Or is there a quality of abiding greatness in the purpose that can inspire others? As much as possible, the person in career transition should align all actions with a humanitarian or spiritual purpose. Wisely chosen goals have the power to inspire others to support actions. Career changers and leaders are in the business of communicating their progress and asking others to support their purpose.

Goals must be communicated with others. When people speak of their goals, those discussion opportunities help to establish a commitment. Strictly personal goals may not need to be communicated with others; however, the work of an emerging leader will usually change others' lives. Common goals ought to be written and discussed. Followers may need to have input into their goals. Communication is not just a one-way process; effective dialogue between parties is essential.

The career-changers I interviewed told me that they worked on long-term goals, fundamental problems, goals related to their customers, and financial goals. In addition, a number of my interviewees told me that the clarity of goals was important for success. An intentional focus of mind follows the creation of clear thinking; this clarity adds mental power to one's action. Clarity is a starting point for solid intentions.

Career-changers understand their long-term goals. Some of their attention is on the long horizon, while still being focused on short-term results. Effective leaders can show followers how their actions for this week support a long-term plan. Leaders expand the mental horizon for their followers, as they look farther downstream.

These leaders in transition used goals to solve problems. Some of the most challenging problems often involve the way that people work together. Resistance toward change often emerges due to the organizational culture; people have expectations and patterns for the way people solve problems together. Emerging leaders solve problems that release workplace energy for innovations and adaptive ways of working.

Leaders envision and propose solutions for their clients. This quality is emblematic of the entrepreneur. They solve problems for the customer. Career-changers frequently think like the entrepreneur, imagining how to make life easier for the client. Many career-changers become entrepreneurs, or were already business-starters before they changed their careers.

Many goals are financial in the world of business and careers. A financial goal supports a clear achievement that can be sustained in the marketplace. Nonprofits and government agencies are like business entities in that financial performance is always important. Financial goals can be measured, scaled, and extended into future periods. Career-changers demonstrate their firm focus on the future by adopting clear financial goals that keep them in the game.

When I talked to emerging leaders about their career changes, goals and paying attention to results were discussed. I learned a great deal from talking to emerging leaders; in this book, I have presented the top five qualities found in a successful leader after a career change. These qualities will serve an emerging leader in any field:

- Connecting with people
- Personal energy
- Learning
- Understanding the context of work
- Clear goals and results

In the next chapter, I will examine a plan of action to help career changers. A person who wants to be a leader in the next phase of his or her life should verify that all five qualities are present and usefully supporting the career-changer. Chapter 13 will present my recommendations for emerging leaders. Chapters 14 and 15 will ask some questions about leadership and the career change process that may help you go further, if you are in transition. Read the epilogue to consider the mythic dimension of changing a career, facing chaos, and becoming a leader.

LESSONS FOR LEADERS

Follow your goals to reach a major life accomplishment.

Set meaningful goals with your colleagues and followers to achieve lasting victories.

Chapter 13 - Your Career Victory

Let's get personal. Throughout the earlier chapters of this book, my attention was directed to other leaders in transition. Are you ready to make your own career transition, too? Let's look at your situation, and the opportunity you have to perform like a leader.

Begin with assessing your situation. How ready are you to step into the wilderness, and face the storm? If you understand the forces around you, you will have a better chance to prevail in the face of uncertainty.

> **DR. STEVE'S TIPS FOR LEADERS**
> You can do it: Work toward your victory!
>
> W. Clement Stone said, "Aim for the moon. That way, even if you miss, you'll be among the stars."
>
> You will never doubt the worth and meaning of your work if you have an awesome victory in your sights.

VICTORY CHANGES EVERYTHING

Don't settle for a modest improvement in your career. Go for a victory. Your career victory should be an occasion to cheer, a recognition that your life has changed forever. You'll know you have a victory when your body is physically excited, your mind cannot stop thinking about what has happened, and you want to tell the important people in your life what happened. A victory changes everything.

You know you have a career victory when:

Your heart sings the success. The career victory touches most people emotionally. The moment is thrilling, and your heart is lifted with joy. You want to pick up the telephone and call someone important in your life. This moment is so good, it has to be shared.

Your mind is aligned with the heart. You are not thinking about the hard work ahead of you, you are thinking about *how great* it is to be working in an area of your strength, appreciated for who you are, and how fulfilled you will be to taking on new challenges.

A career victory **supports your personal vision**. People in career transition should have a detailed vision of their destination. A personal vision might include achievement (become a Wall Street trader) or a lifestyle choice (take recreational travel one month a year). My personal vision includes the work I want to do, and the amount of time that I dedicate to certain work (writing, coaching, and speaking). The victory should bring you closer to the vision. If the victory doesn't support the vision, then evaluate: either change the vision or look for another victory. The victory should serve the vision, and make it more likely.

Don't change your vision too easily; the vision represents the essential you. When you change your vision, you are essentially declaring, "I was wrong about what I saw before." Perhaps you will update your vision, but don't make *convenient* changes in what is important to you. Be intentional and clear about your vision and your victory.

Feel energized. The career victory should be a source of vital energy. You are working in an area of strength, and you feel great doing this work. Work is still work, but when you are energized, you love performing your "thing." You feel like a champion. The victory helps you enjoy your productivity.

The victory involves a stretch. The victory suggests that you have new goals ahead of you. You have to work at it! You don't take this change for granted, as you will have to apply yourself. You are going to have to perform in new areas. You look forward to the challenge. You want the bragging rights that come with this new assignment. The stretch is neither too easy, nor too difficult. You may have to work long hours to get there, and you expect to sweat some; however, you know the goal is worth it.

The victory takes you some place you have never been before. You've moved forward! Your career is partly a journey of discovery, and a victory is a new destination that you have created for yourself. You would not feel victorious if you were doing the same thing as you were two years ago. The career victory is a watershed moment in one's working life, a chance to add a dramatic highlight to your life. The victory brings new perspective to your work and relations with others.

Not every career change is a victory. When you achieve a victory, you'll know it! Your body and mind will rejoice in accord, and you won't have any doubts about your breakthrough. Keep working with hopeful spirits, and your career victory will be yours if you work toward it.

ASSESSMENT

Once you have visualized your victory, you have taken a big step toward its creation. Launch your efforts to victory. Make sure you know where you are starting. Evaluate your current position. Take a fresh view of your situation. Get the facts before you move forward.

Collect data – Add an impartial view of your personality and strengths. Well-designed behavioral assessment tools can help you understand your capacity to change your situation. I recommend that you collect reports using the following three tools:

DISC Profile
StrengthsFinder
Kolbe A Index

These three tools will describe the way you work with other people (*DISC*), the strengths that you have in the way you work (*StrengthsFinder*), and will report on your instincts (*Kolbe A*) in working. Once you have this information, you will be better prepared to make choices about your direction. You will save energy as you move forward, and you will be better equipped to ask for help.

You will not achieve a career victory by yourself. Most of us have earned our victories by working compatibly with other people. Your circle of influence and trusted network will help you go farther. Your assessment will show you how to best rely on the talents of others.

While you will be able to find the DISC and the StrengthsFinder assessments online and through booksellers, you may want to engage a third party coach or career counselor to help you interpret the findings of your assessment. Don't get lost with the information; discover how this information will help you get the results you have dreamed.

Conduct a SWOT Analysis – SWOT stands for strengths, weaknesses, opportunities, and threats. Your behavioral assessment data will help you identify your strengths and weaknesses. Your creative mind will help you establish the opportunities and threats that you will face when you move toward your victory.

Your strengths and weaknesses may be revealed in the assessment that you just completed. Pay attention to the information – perhaps you will understand a blind spot in the way you work now. You may have strengths that are not used in your current career, and now you will have a chance to employ your natural talent. If you see that you have weak areas, reach out to the people who can help you proceed. You may have to reflect on your assessment before you find the meaning for you and your new career.

Think about the horizon ahead, and declare the opportunities and threats in front of you. Name them. Your opportunities are the chances to move ahead faster; the threats will be barriers that may need to be considered. Prepare your mind, know that the world changes regularly, and be aware of changing conditions that will affect your career transition. If you are mentally prepared and focused, your opportunities will help you achieve your victory faster than you thought possible; and your threats will be met realistically with a courageous heart.

Trusted Review – Use the power of your mastermind circle; get help from others. Review your assessment and SWOT analysis with a trusted peer or mentor. Talk about your career victory. Ask for the opinion of the informed people in your life.

You don't have to announce your career change to everyone. Some people in your circle will not be able to help you. Other people are not working to change their lives in the same way you are. There are some people happily stuck in another way of life, and they may see your proposed "career victory" as a threat to their own stable situation.

Seek career advice carefully! If one of your friends hasn't made a major life change, s/he probably isn't ready to help you take your step forward! Share your assessment with people who have experienced the kind of life change that you propose for yourself. For others, let your transformation be a blessed surprise. You need to protect your state of mind from people with a critical attitude.

ACHIEVE MENTAL CLARITY

Make your career victory your intentional goal. Invest in the interior work so your heart, mind, and spirit are in accord; you know your victory, and you are determined to get there. Your mental attitude will be important, especially when the world distracts you from your purpose.

How do you know if you have mental clarity? I suggest that you will have clarity when:

You have a quiet satisfaction with your career victory. Quiet satisfaction means that you don't need to talk about your decision with everyone, only with a trusted few. You are past the point of needing to talk about the victory vision with everyone. You have found a quiet confidence. You are content with the choice. You don't need to find approval from anyone about it. Someone might try to talk you out of your choice; this wouldn't matter. Your clarity will not be disturbed!

You have a mental image of what you are planning to achieve. You have put yourself in the picture, and you see the career victory in action mode. You could paint a picture or make a movie of the victory condition. Color in the details; you are involved in the picture. What more is in the picture?

You can hold this image for two or more weeks, and the victory idea doesn't change except to get more vivid. I held an image of my completed dissertation for over two years. I imagined all the people this dissertation would help and I saw how my doctoral degree would give me career prestige that I wanted. The image never faded for me, even though I faced my challenges. Find the mental clarity to create a stable image for your future.

Create the clarity that you need to support your journey into a transformative world. The clarity will help you arrive at the victory destination.

Know your circle of influence. You know people who can help you step up to a greater level of performance and achievement. Your victory will come sooner–and be more satisfying–if you use the leveraged power of experience. Be wise and selective when revealing your career victory.

Prepare questions for your trusted circle. Your time and connection with them is too valuable to rely on casual discussion. Use your intention and focus to explore the mutual possibilities with your circle of influence.

Some of the questions you might want to ask are: A) Who else should I talk to about my ideas? B) Who has traveled the route ahead of me? C) Do you see any opportunities that I should explore? D) Can you think of any other ways I can help people by my victory? Keep a mutual exchange of benefits within your circle; you are not only there to advance your own interests, you are also there to help others, especially your friends. Offer help to others when appropriate. Be a giving person, and you will find that others willingly give time and resources to you.

Establish your plans. Then add what you have learned through your assessment and from your discussions with your trusted circle. The plans prepare your mind, give you the language of success as you talk to others, and rekindle the determination to make your victory a certainty. You will be stronger as you step into the wilderness, in pursuit of your life victory, if you know that your next goal can be achieved by doing specific actions. Bring this certainty and conviction to your effort.

Your fundamental plan should be your strategic plan. This is the plan that takes you to your victory. Think of your strategy before you commit to details. Consider what you can achieve if you move forward. Understand your milestones, and estimate the amount of effort it will take to reach each position toward your victory. The strategic plan may challenge you to take risks, and increase your knowledge. The strategy is fundamental to other plans.

What will you need to know to earn your victory? Have you settled on a course of learning? The leaders I interviewed made their education a priority. Whether or not you need a new degree, or simply need to build new technical skills, make your important decisions. Decide what you need to learn, where you will get the knowledge, and decide on your timetable. Your learning plan should bring you into contact with an expert, a person who has mastery in what you need to know. Decide to work with a master, and to become an expert yourself. Your learning plan supports your strategic plan, establishes you as a person of distinction, and will help you achieve your victory.

Create a personal brand for yourself. Establish your position in the marketplace. You will want people to see you in a new way, hence, work on changing their perceptions. Your branding plan is an intentional strategy to build new perceptions, and will help you achieve your victory. The plan gives you some control over what people know about you, and will help people change outdated ideas. Consider hiring a branding coach to help you establish and execute your plan. You will want people to notice what you are achieving; the brand will give you a tool for revealing your transformation.

Milestones. If you were a seafaring captain during the age of exploration, you might plan to sail around the coast of Africa to reach the fabled Indies and trade in spices. Before you reached the Indies, you would have several destinations that would bring you closer to the goal. Sailing around the Cape of Good Hope would be an important milestone–one of many–that brings you closer to your destination.

Your voyage of career transformation will also require a journey of exploration. You will not be in control of the external circumstances, just as the sailor does not control the weather. Establish the milestones that bring you closer to your destination. You may have to make landfall and take a breather before you push on to the victory.

Your milestones ought to include your first landfall. You are exercising new skills, working on new behaviors, and cutting ties with your former career. Your internal world is changing. You are evolving a new perception of yourself. Recognize the launch of your career victory by designating a first major milestone. Your efforts may not seem overwhelming if you know that you can get to this milestone.

Experience the positive exhilaration that comes from a real achievement. As you begin, your first major milestone should be the attention of your focus.

Think about a succession of milestones beyond your first. Even before you launch, you should be aware of several "success points" that bring you within range of your career victory. You may decide to change your milestones as you move ahead, or you may discover that another intermediate point becomes a significant challenge that you had not expected. The success points anchor your achievement as you move forward into an uncertain personal destiny.

Work the plans. You've chosen a victory that motivates you. This is an energizing step! Now pay attention to the factors that can drive you off course: a) Fatigue, b) Distraction, and c) A disabling sense of doubt. Make it an objective every day and every week to move closer to at least one of your goals, whether that goal is a strategic, learning, or branding goal. Make the effort. Invest your time and attention to achieving the plans.

Fatigue may halt your progress. Hence, pay attention to your spirit. Everyone can feel fatigue. When we allow ourselves to restore our energy and immune system, we can return stronger, and more capable of moving forward. Don't make important decisions when fatigued. Consciously recognize, "I am not at my strongest today." Do those things that help your body, mind, and spirit return to full power. The world seems a better place after we have been restored. Review your career victory and your assessment, and find the energy that comes from creating an energizing plan!

Distraction can pull you away from your purpose. I am a distractible person, and I find delight in every new thought and possibility. I also realize that if I chase every golden goose, I won't find any golden eggs. Focus is a powerful tool to help me win goals. Delight leads me to distraction, and this state robs me of the career victory that I have planned for myself. I may indeed wander into the land of delight and distraction, yet I am also disciplined to ensure that my goals and objectives are handled first. I have learned that the important choices I have already made must be honored on a daily basis. I face distraction with the confidence that I am working on my most important challenges first.

Doubt can immobilize anyone. We have learned lessons from an early age that tell us, "I'm not good enough," and "I'm not worthy." These messages may come with a silent voice that robs one of inner strength, or the inner voice may speak up with a strident call to STOP! before one falls in a pit with no way out. You cannot silence the voice of doubt. However, you can choose to pay attention to the voice of resolution that helped you prepare your victory statement and plans. Learn to find strength in your assessment and your rational choices. Know that you are bigger than the part of you that doubts yourself.

The voice of doubt and judgment will call you back to your old way of life, if you let it. We all have experienced a limiting inner voice that calls us to return to security. I've talked to many career-changers about their voice of doubt, and I find it works differently for every person. Some career-changers, however, don't identify with that voice. They replace negative thoughts of their direction with a choice to learn, a choice to respond, and a choice to act. Your voice of doubt may never go away entirely, yet it is possible to be transformed on this journey toward leadership. The journey of transformation does not mean that one abandons doubt; it means that one has new sources of strength and inspiration. Take the choice of learning and positive risk-taking.

BEGIN WITH A DREAM

Your career victory should begin with a dream. Support this dream with what you learn about yourself. Your career victory is important; make the effort to create an adaptable plan that supports your journey. Dedicate yourself to continual learning about your new career and to becoming a better leader. The victory should give you many emotional reasons to celebrate. You will be a changed person–more talented, experienced, and knowledgeable–when you get to this destination.

Your circle of influence may help you reach your victory, or they may shower you with reasons never to move ahead. Share your vision and plans only with people who have taken positive risks for themselves, and with whom you are sure of their good will toward you.

> **LESSONS FOR LEADERS**
> *Your dream today can feature you, and can include a shared victory with others.*

Chapter 14 - Questions to Lead the Leaders

Welcome to a lonely and satisfying world. A leader moves other people into a new place. The leader often has no peers; few understand his or her mantle of responsibility.

Who can counsel the leader? Who are the trusted advisors? Since no one has reached this place before, no one is qualified for speaking about the journey and destination. Yet, leaders are social people, and require opportunities to learn with other people. Ultimately, the leader must take direction from his or her vision of the possible future, and listen to the voice of conscience that advises on the rightness of action.

I have found that in my personal journey of work, traveling as a manager to become a leader is indeed lonely. In the mid-90s, I founded a charter school organization, where none had existed before. I moved from working as a senior manager in a child care company–my business operated child care centers in multiple states–to pioneering the start of a charter school organization. I had the benefit of financial backing behind me, but I had no team of colleagues, nor expertise to join me in opening charter schools that would compete with public school classes to the sixth grade. No one I knew had ever run a charter school business before, and the educational establishment treated all charter schools with suspicion. I was on my own.

I knew of no one who had traveled this journey before me. No one could give me advice as an organization creator, as a person offering a vision to others, or as a person establishing a culture that would last for years. I had to invent my own path.

> **DR. STEVE'S TIPS FOR LEADERS**
> Be open to changes that will transform you.
> Understand that you have experiences and knowledge that will help you succeed in your new career.
> Have a courageous heart.
> Examine your thinking.
> Seek counsel going forward.

Leaders must have a courageous heart. They move forward, often with accountability to financial partners or other business leaders. They must challenge others to do their best while working in terrain new to them.

Teachers are very special to me. They dedicate years of their lives to serving others. As they mature, many teachers get frustrated with the institutional rules that come from working with a large school district. I have talked to dozens of teachers who continue to transform their lives after working in a classroom, by finding ways to serve their communities. Teachers who begin new careers in business and non-profit leadership often are challenged by their roles without an institution as formal as a school district to hold them accountable. They feel the internal drive to make a difference, while working on their own terms and pace is new to them. At the same time, teachers moving into an entrepreneurial role often discover how much they depended on the many support services that a large institution provided for them. The new entrepreneur often must fill many new job roles in his or her schedule.

Lois made a successful transition from public teaching into private employment. She now considers herself a leader in the community, helping improve the lives of senior citizens. Lois has learned to work as a sales professional, while working in service for the elderly. The transformation in the way Lois works is massive.

Lois's work history included work as a third grade teacher. She worked for several years as a drug counselor, and then returned to education as an assistant principal for an alternative high school. She earned a master's degree in counseling, and then worked as a reading teacher. Her work history demonstrates a profound interest in helping other people.

Now a parent of adult children, Lois considered retirement five years ago. She asked herself, "How can I stay productive?" Looking inward, she decided that she did not like the idea of full retirement. She attended a seminar through a life education institution. She was challenged to create community blood drives, set significant goals for blood collection, and work with other volunteers to make a difference. Lois was changed by this project; her heart and mind were fully engaged by the challenge and purpose. She was determined to create a lasting impact in the community, and leave a stronger blood drive program after her volunteer stewardship ended.

"I was on fire, I was unstoppable," Lois told me. She gained a new perspective on how she could change things. Lois told me that she decided to "make a beeline for the results" she wanted. "I want to contribute more and more." She discovered that when she knew the purpose of what she was working for, she could achieve great things. She proved that to herself with her community blood drive, and now she wants to make the world a better place for senior care.

Lois is proud to be working on a commission basis today. She feels free to help people in the way that she believes will make the most difference. Her concern for the well-being of senior citizens–often the parents of her peers–is apparent. She told me how committed she is to helping people find new living arrangements, and she loves being paid when a placement is through her company. Getting paid isn't her top concern though. She wants to see people helped through her service. "My perspective on life has changed," Lois told me.

Lois is representative of what I saw with so many career-changers with whom I spoke. Their career change was more than a change in duties. It represented a new way of thinking about work. The career change is a crucible that transforms people down to an essential character level. Many career-changers become leaders because of a passionate connection to an important idea. Thoughts are powerful catalysts for creating a meaningful new life.

I learned about the careers and leadership experience of the men and women I interviewed recently. They had good ideas about the change they had worked through, and were pleased to share their thoughts with me. I ended every interview with the same question, hoping to bring their advice and insight to future career-changers in ways that I hadn't expected: "What questions should I ask people changing careers when I talk to them? What is important for emerging leaders to know?"

Here are some of the questions that I heard from the leaders I talked to for this project–the same people you have been reading about in this book.

WHAT RESOURCES HAVE YOU TAPPED INTO?

Look beyond what you know. I shudder when I hear the comment, "Insanity is doing the same thing over and over again and expecting different results." To get results, one needs to be persistent. Often, one learns and is changed by the act of persistent effort. It is NOT insanity to repeat actions if one is learning and becoming more proficient in the process. We can all improve our chances for success by talking to new people, finding new markets, and asking better questions.

You do not have to know everything or have all the resources in order to change your career and become a leader. Others will help you on your journey. Have you asked for help? Have you asked about what is available? How much effort goes into your learning plan, in an effort to explore beyond what you know?

We all have blind spots. Make an effort to discover yours. Important resources that will speed you forward may lay only three phone calls away. Ask about what is out there to help you.

WOULD YOU BE OPEN TO NEW CHANGES IN YOUR LIFE?

Is your door to discovery open? Alternatively, are you letting fears keep you trapped into the same line of work? I encourage you to explore the changes that will propel you forward. Make an intentional decision to explore the possibilities that change can bring. Adopt the mindset that says, "I welcome positive changes! I am ready to drop useless, unproductive habits."

Face the changes gladly, with a heart that smiles at your new opportunities. Be open; eliminate any resistance for letting positive change in your life. Yes, you may have to walk through the doorway of uncertainty. Have confidence in your talents and resources to create a better place in your life.

DO YOU KNOW WHAT MOTIVATES THE PEOPLE IN YOUR LIFE?

Everyone is different. Some people are activated by an idea; other people need to be convinced with data. A skillful leader treats people in their circle as unique, with a constellation of special factors that apply especially to them. Find out what it takes to light fire in the minds and hearts of your circle.

I don't believe leaders directly motivate others. Leaders can destroy motivation, and they can encourage others to be motivated. Motivation comes from within, not from another person. Leaders can help followers create their personal motivation if they have earned the right to influence their friends.

Leaders can help followers create their own motivation through *appreciative inquiry*, and through *responsible questions*. By appreciative inquiry, we can create alignment with other people. Appreciation is a position of compassionate understanding. Inquiry is a process of exploration. When followers sense that a leader has genuine interest in their well-being, powerful collaborations may be created.

Responsible questions offer a guided exploration into the attitude and intention into the followers' connections. Leaders must be courageous in asking followers about their reasons for action, or the failure to act. When the leader applies questions without a judging tone, and has established a field of appreciation, the follower may respond with interest and growing motivation.

You cannot motivate your followers. You can inspire others to join you, and your authentic connection with their individual needs can help to create this connection. Appreciate your followers' needs and be courageous in asking your circle of influence to make a commitment to your vision. Your trusted followers may respond with their own motivation; be grateful for this connection. If it happens, your followers have designated you as a leader!

HOW ARE YOU BUILDING YOUR SUPPORT SYSTEM?

I don't know of anyone who has become successful by themselves. Whenever a courageous person accomplishes something significant, other people have been around to make it happen. The people in your life can support you if you let them, and if you recognize their special contribution to you. Look for diversity of strengths. Look for people with more experience than you.

You may need to build a team later on, or you may need an introduction. Stay connected. Remain a compassionate and authentic person while you follow your strategic plan. Let the people in your support system know where you are going, and ask them for their ideas about how to get their faster.

Don't be just a taker. Reciprocate. Help the people in your support team know that you give back attention, energy, time, and resources. Get a reputation as the kind of person who generates more than you take from others, and you will be surrounded by caring support. The people you support will look after you, and keep you from hurting yourself, if they can possibly do it.

WHAT QUALITIES ABOUT YOU SPAN BOTH CAREERS?

This book has been all about the transformation of a person in one career into a person who leads in a new career. Your transformation does not have to be a rejection of your past, however! You have learned so much of value in all your assignments. Even when the last job was negative, and bosses have been bullies, you have become more capable.

You will need the best aspects of your earlier career as you move into new work. You have cultivated discipline and attention, knowledge and relationships. It is likely that most of these factors will be necessary factors in the new part of your life.

Do you value what you have done before? After I left my career managing child care centers, I wanted to reject all aspects of my earlier work. I couldn't wait to reinvent myself! Don't be as hard on yourself as I was. Remember that you have been a productive, intelligent person. Bring your strong qualities forward, but with the enhanced knowledge and experience that you bring to your new career.

As I entered my transition, I looked back at my role as the general manager for ten child care centers, schools, and self-storage businesses. I had managed a number of people, and maintained a positive relationship throughout. I documented a training program for new managers, and created a recruitment program for new teachers. I had managed an accounting system and introduced mini-computers into a business that had operated completely on paper records in the past. My strengths were my connections to people, understanding of the learning process at work, and applying technology to changes in the workplace.

Use your period of transition to look at the best qualities that are part of you. When you take away the old job, what remains that is valuable? Be proud of your essential strengths, and find ways to put these qualities to work in your future. Use your experience and strength as stepping stones through your transition.

WHAT ELSE IS IMPORTANT IN THE TRANSITION PERIOD?

The transition period might be treacherous, but you have a strategic map to help you navigate the route ahead! If you have followed the suggestions in the previous chapters, you are on your way to being an influential leader, or even more of one, with a solid map for your journey. The benefit of the transition period is that you have the greatest opportunity to make changes at the present. You can change your schedule, launch new learning programs, and take calculated risks. Although the transition period may not be "fun," it may offer the prepared leader a number of opportunities. Are you paying attention?

The transition period is an excellent period to prepare your mind. I recommend keeping a journal, a place to document the passing thoughts and reflections about your journey. Keep note of the opportunities for you to explore.

What else is important? Your mind should be aware, and perceptive. Invest in the important relations in your life. Where can you get more information about the world ahead? What will people be saying about your career in a year's time? Think and explore the undefined; become the master of the uncertain future by seizing the landmarks ahead while your secure competitors are still thinking about their next vacation. Capture the forward position!

The place of transitions is often uncertain and chaotic. Discover what is important. Pay attention to actions and their consequences. Learn the nature of this transitional world, and you can be the master of the transitional world. Help others to create their lives anew.

WHAT ARE THE THOUGHT PROCESSES THAT BROUGHT YOU HERE?

All actions began with thoughts. If you have changed careers, or you are working on a career change, you transformed your thinking from, "I like it right here," to "I think I can do better than this." Your questions to yourself are the conscious guidance system for a life built on knowledge, habits, secure choices, and attitudes. The questions we ask ourselves can point us in new directions and new careers.

You probably asked yourself some important questions. Questions can be extremely powerful in starting a life change. Your questions might have included,

> "Would I be more satisfied doing something else?"
> "When should I make a change in my work?"
> "Should I change my career gradually, or change everything all at once?"
> "What do I need to do to be successful?"

Keep asking yourself questions. Questions prepare your mind for action, and signal your mind to be aware of changes. Do you notice the questions that you ask yourself? Your questions precede your actions.

Have you ever moved through a dark room, and reached out to feel a wall, a chair, or something familiar? Career changers move through the dark room called "transition." The questions we ask during the transition are like putting a hand out in the dark, finding the boundaries and the path without obstruction. Good questions tune our mind into the present.

Ask yourself questions without judging yourself. Instead of asking yourself questions that put yourself down ("Why did I think I could be an engineer? I don't have the smarts for that!") ask questions that help you examine the challenge without internal ridicule–for example, "What would I have to learn to be a good engineer?"

Ask questions that help you learn more about your new career, or how you will respond to changes. Think about the questions you need to answer to move forward with confidence.

After you ask internal questions, do you respond with action? Do you work up the courage to act? Understand your own thought processes, and how you generate the willpower to act.

> **LESSONS FOR LEADERS**
> *Keep asking yourself questions. Take control of your thoughts, and manage your emotions.*
>
> *Learn the necessary lessons in your new career.*

Chapter 15 - Some Thoughts on Changing Your Behavior

Your mind can change your behavior. The choices we make can lead us to action–action that can make us more productive. A productive life can help any person live with more satisfaction, and can increase one's standard of living.

Leaders have often made a shift in their thinking. That shift moves one from the center of the world, and places other people in the valued center. Leaders don't make themselves small in their minds; they add other people to their constellation of importance. The shift is like the world shift in astronomy that moved the earth from the center of the universe to a broader view that places the sun in the center. Leaders value the importance of other people in their galaxy of social connections. Leaders understand that a better world is not "all about me."

To change your career, you must change your behavior. You may become a leader in the process. You will need to allow your mind to evolve as you create your change.

> **DR. STEVE'S TIPS FOR LEADERS**
> Profound change begins with change from your inner world. Look within.
> Ask yourself, "How ready am I to make the important changes?"
> At some point you will come to a choicepoint—a life-changing bridge that must be crossed or you will not advance. Prepare yourself, and choose the way forward across the bridge. Your victory lies ahead.

ARE YOU REALLY READY TO MAKE CHANGES, OR ARE YOU FLIRTING WITH THE CONCEPT?

It is OK to look into a career change, and not yet be fully committed to the journey! Most important change starts with a wondering period. A consideration phase is typical, and it indicates that the conditions are not right for committed action. Know your own mind; if you are not passionate about launching your next career, you are not ready to cut the safety lines with your old work.

A teaching from Zen philosophy is appropriate here: "Don't wobble." If you are considering a career change, that's great! Get more information, and make a decision when you are ready. Don't pretend that you are making a change, because you are still in the consideration phase. On the other hand, if you are ready to change, then move forward. Cut the ties that hold you to the past. Do not hang onto the security of your old world. Take action to move forward, even if the action begins with consulting your network and developing your strategic map. Be committed, if that is your choice!

Don't wobble between the position, "I'm considering," and, "I'm committed." Find the clarity, and know your position. Your clarity of knowledge and action will help you achieve your big goals.

DO YOU UNDERSTAND THAT INTERNAL CHANGE IS NECESSARY TO CHANGING YOUR CAREER?

You will not be successful in creating a satisfying career change if you remain the same person who holds the old career. You must create yourself anew–learning new skills, communicating in the way of a business leader or technical expert, and handling your time differently. The career-changer must also leave behind unproductive or non-essential habits that won't support the career change. Find the focus that takes you forward, accept the new parts of your character, and abandon other parts.

The journey through the transitional world arrives as a shock to most career changers, and it colors one's emotional response to future encounters. Our internal view of the world changes, and we usually expand our emotional intelligence. This change frequently hastens our development as a leader.

Expect to be more influential and connected as you move through your transition. These qualities of a leader come at a cost to our psyche. The process of being changed may feel like a wound. The pain may be sharp; however, it does not have to be disabling. The experience almost always changes one's character at a bedrock level.

WHAT DO YOU HAVE TO CHANGE TO LAUNCH YOUR CAREER MOVE?

Examine your position, and review your strategic map. Your world will not be the same once you commit to moving forward. You may have to give up some aspect of security from your old world before you can make progress in the new. What will you change?

You don't have to abandon your security completely, but you will have to take some intelligent risks. Make a conscious change in your working situation. Commit your mind to move forward.

You may have to learn a lot to get to your career victory. Young children hesitate to give up crawling before they master walking, and yet no one regrets taking their steps forward. Once a child learns to walk, crawling is abandoned. In your new career, you may leave behind old crawling behavior in favor of sprinting ahead… when you are ready.

If your decision to launch your new career is clear, then change your game. Reach for your dream. Accept that you are leaving the old and comfortable behind.

HAVE YOU CROSSED THE EMOTIONAL BRIDGE? HAVE YOU DECIDED?

Think of your journey as a bridge between your familiar world of your current career and the career victory that you dream about. The journey requires emotional experience as well as committed action. Even to make the journey forward, you must cross the bridge in your mind, and be ready to act.

If you haven't "crossed the bridge" at an emotional level, then you probably aren't going to act immediately. Not until you see the benefits are worth the risks, or you are left with no other good choices, will you land on the side of decision. Before you cross the bridge entirely, you are in the land of "decision consideration." There is nothing wrong with that!

Once you have crossed the bridge, your mind is made up; your direction is forward. Don't look back. Make intelligent choices, and pay attention to your security until you are willing to sever ties with your current situation. Think strategically, and act in accordance with opportunities.

Look at how you made the decision to cross that emotional bridge. Understand yourself, and the process that you took to clarify your intention. As a potential leader in a new field, your perception and awareness about your emotional space makes you a capable influencer of others! Your expertise about your inner world may give you insights into working with colleagues.

CHANGE IS TOUGH. ARE YOU WILLING TO BE DISCIPLINED?

Self-discipline helps any leader maintain a stable platform during change. I find discipline in the routines I keep toward work, in my dedication to my gym time, and to my relentless focus on writing. You will find discipline in other activities. Understand that your discipline creates a toughness of character, increasing your chances of successfully moving through transition to a new career. Understand and celebrate your discipline.

You can bolster your self-confidence by working in a disciplined manner. I found that I could stay focused on five years of advanced study online while working in my day job and supporting my family. I wrote papers, conducted original research, and presented my ideas in live forums. This knowledge of my proven work habits helped me take on other projects with confidence. I know that I can apply myself to my chosen work with predictable and constant effort. I have earned this confidence. You have probably met major life goals in a similar disciplined way that reminds you of what you are capable of doing.

Your discipline inspires others. You demonstrate to others that leaders work hard. Speak positively and with expectation to others about their performance. Be consistent with your own work habits, and encourage new goals which push forward from those whom you influence. If your behavior matches your words, you may inspire action!

Change can lead to uncertainty, and conditions of doubt sap human potential. Disciplined work habits strengthen the achievements of leaders and their followers. When you discipline yourself to work conscientiously, responsibly, and rigorously, you create a tonic against the draining effects of change.

Change is tough. Discipline and learned patterns of behavior help anyone concerned with achievement push on, determined to make it through the darkness of transition. Expect to be hit by the forces of change. Build the internal toughness needed to persist through to your career victory by following your strategic, learning, and branding plans with discipline.

WHAT ARE YOUR SUPPORT SYSTEMS FOR CHANGING?

Support systems for a career-hanger may include your family, people who will help you learn, people who will help you with your strategic plan, and people who will help you stay positive and keep moving. I think the idea of the hardy entrepreneur who braves change and transition alone is a myth; everyone gets support. Know and support your support systems. They increase the chances that you get to the finish line. They are valuable to you.

Keep your support systems healthy. Talk to people, and help others whenever possible. The flow of energy should work in all directions with all connections. If you are not sharing your special gifts with others, you may find that your support declines just when you need it. Don't be an opportunist. Support the people who support you.

Most systems are in a state of growth or contraction. If you find that your support system is not growing, then you have work to do. Put time and attention into your support circles. Help them expand outward. Of course, this means your connected responsibilities to others will also grow. Keep the channels of connection vital, strong, and growing.

Think of your support systems as a living entity, like a vine that spreads out in many directions. Don't treat this support system as a thing; treat it as a part of healthy professional living. You are connected to the many people who support you. You may not realize the myriad ways in which you support others when they need it. Understand that this dynamic connection helps you advance in the condition of change.

> **LESSONS FOR LEADERS**
>
> *Look at your mental attitude. Whether you are in growth or contraction, your state will often depend on the choices you make. You have the power to change your mind, direct your life, and leave the world a better place.*

Chapter 16 - Are You Becoming a Leader Yet?

Do you have to become a leader to have a successful career change? Many of my readers have different needs. Some readers are interested because they believe that becoming a leader is a reflection of financial success. Others are already leaders, and want to become more effective in what they do. Some, like me, are interested in continual personal transformation.

I believe that as we cope with change, expand our social network, and gain more professional knowledge and experience, most of us end up acting like leaders. The leader typically has more experience than the other players have on a team, and the leader has a good emotional skill-set that allows persuasion and influence to work smoothly and equitably. Good bosses are not an accident; leaders have experienced a great deal.

I know that not everyone wants to become a leader. There is no half-step toward emerging a leader; responsibilities and requirements drive a leader's actions. Once one begins to think of oneself as a leader, one is engaged in the process. Becoming a leader is a meaningful journey. Career-changers often see a new world as they expand their choices.

> **DR. STEVE'S TIPS FOR LEADERS**
> Leaders are not made by accident. We intentionally move in that direction. The circumstances of the world may "encourage" an emerging leader, but the heavy work of change is a personal decision.
>
> If you are choosing to act as a leader, celebrate your decision to be a responsible force for good in the world.

Please don't become a fake leader. If you feel an authentic pull in this direction, this book may help you serve as a leader more capably. If not, well, the world has seen enough tyrants and office dictators; I don't enjoy sharing the word "leader" with people driven by power and self-serving achievement needs. Look for a higher purpose, a "pull" for an important reason. If you know what this reason is, then I don't think you will be a bad leader. Let your work be pulled forward by the need to make this world a nicer place.

However, if you have doubts about your capabilities as a leader, this book may help you perform well. Doubt and awareness of limitation is common with people driven by a great cause. We are all less than perfect. Leaders with transformational purpose are willing to make the journey even with knowledge of personal flaws.

I am in the midst of transformation too. I am a committed lifelong learner; I dedicate some portion of my time to mentoring and coaching others. I believe that I can be most effective if I keep myself sharp, especially when working with careers and leadership strengths in the dynamically changing 21st century. My investment of time in learning and connecting is deeply satisfying and helps me keep my perceptive vision fresh and renewed.

Won't you share your ideas with me? I believe that human experience is something that can be shared, person-to-person, writer-to-reader, blogger-to-community, and all parties are enriched when this happens. I am driven to help other people become effective leaders, and remove some of the doubt and confusion that accompanies a journey through the storm. Human experience shared with a good heart is a transformational medicine.

LESSONS FOR LEADERS

Even a person who has many doubts can be a great leader. In fact, the doubting mind may actually help a leader look deeper into a situation.

It does take courage to act, and leaders move forward in spite of reservations and doubts.

Epilogue - The Storm and the Well

An intrepid traveler is interrupted on his journey because of a momentous storm. Winds, heavy rain, dark skies, and threatening sounds assail the traveler. In unfamiliar country, the traveler seeks shelter wherever possible, and rests body and mind. Even partial, rustic protection will help the traveler gain a rest while the storm interrupts a safe sojourn.

While writing this book, exploring the world of career change and emerging leaders through discussion with leaders in transition, I imagined a metaphorical story of the storm and the well. Career-changers, like all emerging leaders, enter a dangerous period of transition. The imagery of the traveler grabbed my imagination.

The career-changer has launched a new phase of life voluntarily, just as the traveler proceeds to a new part of the world. The storm interrupts one's easy passage. All phases of life can be touched by a storm, as the storm offers the powerful violence of the natural elements reorganizing the forces of the world. The person in transition and emerging leaders both seek to create a new order; the storm is an encounter with power and fury. Change does not come easily!

After the storm, the traveler feels a sense of liberation. Joy! A liberated spirit is no longer pounded by powerful forces buffeting in various directions. One's soul is lifted. Liberation of the prepared mind allows one to progress after the storm, in a rare moment of clear passage for one who is ready for the shift in energy.

Moving forward, the traveler encounters a well of sweet water. Invited to drink from the well, the traveler is refreshed, and further restored to wholeness. The career-changer and emerging leaders may also find their source of sustenance, a well of knowledge that aids further progress.

The well is a source for refreshment for the person in transition. Once discovered, the well continues to provide clean water and fresh insight. This well refreshes from an internal source. Even though the traveler has moved on, the well is available, as though a delivery truck of fresh water always brings water to the place where the emerging leader needs it! The well invites those who drink from its source to return again and again.

Unlike wells found in towns or desert oases, the well of knowledge and leadership is not bounded by space. Once invited to drink from the well, distance is not a problem. The community of people in transition and emerging leaders can offer this refreshing liquid of a transformed life, no matter where the person is staying.

The leader soon learns that the well is the property of the community, and that he has an obligation to add to the wisdom held within. Leaders bring their own vital source to the well, and contribute to the knowledge, confidence, and inspiration to those who drink later.

FEARS AFTER THE STORM

After the storm, some people bound forward, embracing new opportunities. Others hold back, reluctant to take a risk. The choice of a positive risk in the direction of a dream is the indicator of a successful transition.

Why are people fearful of change? Robert Sapolsky, in his 2004 book, Why Zebras Don't Get Ulcers, tells us that two factors associated with change restrict people: fear of the unknown, and fear of loss of control. With these fears felt at decision moments, some people seize up, reluctant to take action. The person who can take even a modest action forward has an advantage in dispelling fears.

Replace the fear of the unknown with a vision of an improved future.

Replace the fear of the unknown with a vision of an improved future. The career-changer has at least the start of a vision that he or she works toward creating. A leader ought to be a conscious advocate of a transformational vision. People in transition can make a decision to support the vision and feed it with hope, wonder, and possibility. The end of the storm is a great time to bring your vision forward, and share it with others.

People in transition give up control plus face the fear of the unknown. The fear associated with giving up control is a message of scarcity: "I will not be secure in my future. My controlling behavior helps me protect myself from hunger and homelessness." After the storm has passed, the person in transition would do well to reach for the next stage of life, and leave old control systems behind. This act requires an act of faith. A deep personal knowledge of one's values and vision help generate the faith needed to move forward.

The future is a product of the imagination; in order to make it real, old controls must be turned off. Examine your old restrictive thinking. Perhaps it is time to discard it. Creative effort must be applied to the new future. The feeling of liberation refreshes one's psyche as the old controls are no longer important to one's ego.

IN TRANSITION, AFTER THE STORM

There comes a time when the storm begins to subside. Career-changers, look up! It may be time to act.

During the storm, the person in transition is pummeled. Life challenges threaten one's security. Self-confidence ebbs, and one is never sure if the path ahead will ever become clear. Doubts may arise. The career-changer feels pulled back to the secure past. During the hard period, the person in transition should seek shelter, and gain protection from the challenges.

Under shelter, the career-changer should take only modest advances forward. This is a good time to prepare for future action. The career-changer may wisely use the time of the storm to collect supplies, review strategy, and learn about the nearby environment. Because the storm is an unpredictable period of powerful wind and precipitation, the career -hanger should not go too far from shelter.

At some point, however, the storm will subside. The shift may be subtle at first. Observe the change: Has the pressure lifted? Is the clamor down? Be careful that the calmer period is sustained, and not just the eye of the hurricane. Venture out, and perceive the storm. Look toward its center. Is it leaving you? All things change.

When the storm is departing, another phase of the career-changer's life may begin. The time for action commences. Understand that others will be timid after the storm has left. This is the time for opportunity; seize the day! Use the wisdom and planning that you have prepared during the storm. The new calm offers less competition, and more, clearer roads. The opportunity is favorable for fast action.

Action after the storm should be swift. You can gain ground without large challenges. Exploit the opportunity to move forward. During the storm, the time is not favorable for action, and now others may tremble and fear action while the emerging career-changer sets up shop.

While the storm is subsiding, examine your problems. Do you need a solution? This may be a time of breakthrough. You have persisted through the frightening storm, and while others are recovering in a safe room, you are looking at your situation with fresh eyes. This period, after the storm, may be the moment that you need to find your solution.

Have confidence in yourself, and in your ability to solve problems. The storm may not be the right time to exercise your strengths. Be patient, and the period after the storm departs may be your sweet spot. Trust that you have a connection with soulful energy and wisdom. The solution that you looked for may no longer be elusive. The end of the storm creates an opportunity for people of good will, especially those in transition. Step forward with confidence.

The nature of leadership work is to travel through fears and dangers, and bring others successfully forward. Jack Welch wrote, "Leadership is seeing opportunity in tough times." Leaders make the most of the difficult phase.

We all experience tough times. For career-changers, I believe that there is a period like a storm in one's life, a phase when certainty and confidence seems to slip away. The person in transition must step forward, perhaps following a life-gripping dream. The tough times may sap one of courage and the transitioner may feel pulled back and forward. For many of us, emotions cycle through alternating periods of giddiness and despair. Even the strongest among us feel the chill of the storm.

Some among us are potential leaders. These people look to the conditions in the world, and perceive opportunities. Leaders suffer like others, yet are able to sell a vision of a better future, seemingly just ahead.

If the storm hasn't touched your life yet, be sure that you will face it sometime in the near future. Prepare your bold initiative to advance your dream and agenda. Take advantage of the numb feeling that others will feel as the storm lifts.

OK, so the storm has lifted? Make a quick assessment – what has changed? Earlier plans may need to be revised, because new forces are at play. You have your dream, your plans, and now you must put yourself into the cold, wet world. You may have to wander through debris and confusion left behind by the storm. Need to change your plans? Good. Adapt. Stay constant with the vision of what you are creating, and find a way to execute your ideas in this changing world.

THE STORM ROCKS US; IT IS NOT THERE FOR COMFORT

Before the storm subsides, the spirit is drained. The nature of the storm is a psychic battering against one's energy and confidence.

Have confidence that the storm is not permanent, and the spirit will again soar.

For a person in transition, and for all emerging leaders, learn to sense the shift in the storm's fury. The storm does not touch all people equally; especially for a person in transition, the security of the past is gone, and the storm rocks one's world with mighty impact.

My friend Robert LeGendre taught me, "Just remember . . . on your darkest day the sunrise will always follow." The storm racks one with doubts, and some will turn back. If you are an observer of life forces, then you will recognize that all things change. The storm is a temporary condition, a trying time which is also part of the cycle of change. Given enough time, the storm will move on.

The storm is not a heavenly gift to comfort us; the storm helps us focus the inner spirit. We can use the intensity of the storm to organize our priorities and review our intentions. The storm can help us collect our mental thoughts and direct our behaviors toward the leader's vision and the intended career change.

THE AUTHENTIC LEADER IN THE STORM

A calm demeanor helps settle nervous followers. I advocate that leaders should always be authentic, so what happens if the leader is nervous and jumpy? The nervous leader doesn't inspire followers during this time. Better to find the calmness before speaking to the followers. Don't fake a calm center, as followers detect frauds easily.

Leaders and career-changers can expect to suffer many storms of life, complete with shaking, thunder-and-lightning experience that rattles one's confidence. We want our leaders to show us confidence, yet sometimes the prodigious nature of the storm shakes us up. A leader is expected to proclaim during the storm, "Here we stay!" or "Onward through the storm!" The leader may suffer from a lack of confidence even as followers are looking for direction.

The leader has an advantage going for him: vision, and experience. Vision shows the leader that something wonderful lies ahead. The clarity of the vision varies among leaders, yet the amount of detail, light, and insight into the visionary details can provide a counterpoint to the storm. Followers can integrate the vision into their reckoning, understanding that the storm is not the only reality. A vision creates options.

A leader also has life experience going for him or her. We expect the leader to understand the nature of the storm. The leader has been there before. The leader knows that all storms pass. Understanding that comes from previous experience helps the leader authentically advise followers.

The leader may also know how to return to center quickly. Shaken, go to center. Shaken twice, back twice. The leader receives knowledge from the well of experience. The leader continually learns and proceeds after moving through turbulent working space. This cycle of upheaval should comfort the leader so that calm space can be achieved again. Cultivate a calm inner space. Make the return to center part of the authentic journey of the leader.

My colleague, Barbara Greene, has written that "If you appear confident and at ease in your own skin, you can go far. If you remain calm during the inevitable storms, you will go farther." Leaders frequently do go farther. Their confidence has been earned through past encounters with the storm, and a connection with inner spirit that endures through challenging moments. When a leader with authentic grounding in life challenges faces the storm, he or she helps followers regain their composure and proceed at the right moment.

LIBERATION AFTER THE STORM

The career-hanger has passed through a life crisis while traveling through the storm. The storm is a powerful external buffeting of forces; internally the person in transition feels pulled backward, forward, and contemplates distracting new directions.

The person in transition is weakened during the storm because one's inner confidence is robbed of reassurance.

"In all of nature, no storm can last forever," said Wayne Dyer. The storm is our personal encounter with turbulence, and this, too is fated to move on. Change is universal; even the storm leaves our life.

After the storm comes a lifting of the spirit. A liberating spirit enters softly, filling the inner world of the person in transition. This experience of liberation supports the actions of the emerging leader.

Experience the liberation. Open your eyes, and breathe deeply. Pause, and consult your center of experience. Can you sense what has changed?

The liberation is your permission to move. Don't hesitate. You have put all the pieces together. Check the landscape that you work in. The storm held you back, and now the danger has moved elsewhere. This is your opportunity to claim the goal!

Test your limits. The liberation means that you have been freed of old restrictions. Have you heard the story of circus elephants that are tethered at a young age, and grow up never testing the rope that has become merely symbolic? The older elephant is quite capable of breaking its restraining rope. Nevertheless, the elephant has established a pattern of life in which it never challenges its restriction. The time of liberation, after the storm, is your call to test those old handcuffs. The restrains that bound you before may no longer hold you! Determine to go where you couldn't before. Challenge your thinking.

Claim your energy. Have you rested during the storm, using the period as a chance to check your resources and build your strategy? Excellent. Now check your system. Alert your muscles and your productive mind: This is my time to go. System, get ready. The passing of the storm is your opportunity to sprint.

Call your posse. If you are changing careers, you will be stronger if you alert the people on your side. Send out a press release, make some phone calls, and update your Facebook wall. Stay connected;

ask some critical questions. "I'm moving ahead now; can I count on you?"

THE LIBERATED SPIRIT: STAY OPEN

Immediately after the storm, with an open mind, the creative spirit is touched with possibility. Imagine the chains removed from a man in bondage, and the career transitioner feels his mental and physical powers allowed to surge forward without restraint.

The mind opens following the storm's departure. During the storm, mental energies have been battered, and now they are released. With hope and focus, the spirit of fresh possibility can exult with the joy of expression. The open mind may feel its liberation tentatively at first; with no opposition, it can express itself vividly and boldly. Feel the wave of change.

Keep the mind open. If you have made a transition, do not be in a hurry to put new restraints on your mind and spirit! This is the time when your spirit can stretch to new places. The natural feeling of opposition has departed with the storm. Your old patterns will restore you to a feeling of security. This is not the time to seek security! Try out new patterns. Let your spirit delight in the opportunity to expand. There will be no resistance after the storm has left, at least not immediately. Experiment with the potential you have to create your dream.

Recognize this opportunity as a favorable period. Your spirit has been yearning for this liberation, for this permission to soar. Keep an observant mind; what can you learn while the storm has subsided? Your spirit may be giddy with the opportunity, and this is a joyful feeling. At the same time, learn from your situation. The moment is favorable now, and all things change. What does the new balance of forces teach you?

Understand this state of mind. Your restraints are removed, and your spirit joyfully explores the playground. In time, new forces will be in place. Make this a goal: Keep your spirit liberated. Even while others seek to confine you, preserve internal freedom.

THE RESILIENT SPIRIT

The calm after a storm is not a permanent respite. The storm has passed, and a new kind of equilibrium will be established. New forces move into the workplaces, and these tend to balance themselves out. Businesses and organizational ventures must learn to survive in the midst of a new configuration of power and pressure.

The person in transition may feel lifted by the departure of the storm, and the spirit feels empowered to act. With the advantage of fresh perception and a mind willing to challenge the way things were, the person in transition can seize opportunities. However, the feeling of lift from the spirit may be a temporary benefit. New forces will establish themselves, forcing the potential leader to adapt and find new ways of working. The respite from the storm is not a permanent condition, and the person in transition must renew personal energy and optimism.

I recommend that career-changers and emerging leaders seek the well. In the pre-industrial world, the well was a place that one turns to for water, the fundamental nourishment. The leadership well is a supportive resource for the spirit and intellect of the person in transition. Even after the forces of the challenging world refreeze in a new configuration, the well will endure as a source of inspiration.

Tend to your spirit. Find your well, and drink deeply. Understand that the storm enters life regularly, and you are given the chance to advance through your preparation and resilient energy. Challenging times will return. Regardless, the spirit may need to hear sincere appreciation and words that lift. Your well will give you access to balm for troubles, strategies for advancement, and new ways of perceiving a complex world. Honor your connection to the well. Your life will be positively changed if you drink from the source.

A LOOK AT YOUR NETWORK AFTER THE STORM

The storm is over. Look around. You have arrived at a place of (relative) safety. The period after tumult is a good time to reconsider the way you work. Begin with this: What are your relationships with other people like? You have gone through a transformation. You have drunk from the well of knowledge. Don't treat people the same way you did before. Now is the time to connect with people intentionally. Live the transformation. What is going to change?

Think about who you are. What is your essence now? Have you grown in the last six months? Perhaps you have new insight, new gifts of service to offer the people around you. Look at your relationships with gratitude. Leaders are allowed the fulfilling opportunity to change the world through the relationships of good people.

Look deeper to the people in your trust radius. Examine them as a leader would: see potential, understand challenges. Make your connection more intense; allow more energy to flow between you.

Is this the right time to expand your trust radius? You have new radiance to share–part of the crucible experience that you have gone through. Are you willing to enter the dance of connection with people you have never trusted before? Don't look at people and think, "This is how she will be useful to me." Invest the time and effort to look at people with more depth, "I see the greatness within her." The investment of trust is not always rewarded; however, I believe that overall, it is worth the risk to extend trust. Use your intuition. You may not want to be vulnerable with everyone.

More storms will arrive in your life. Your connections will help you advance in the face of new challenges, and you will help others as well. Use the gift of new insight and trust in yourself to offer meaningful relationships while the storm has departed. Your connections give you new ability to serve others; they empower you with possibility.

After the storm, some people will be in distress. Help them. Others will barely feel the same winds that challenged you. Isn't it remarkable how we feel the effects of the same conditions, and our spirits respond differently, depending on our context? The storm creates openness in some, and resistance in others. The expanding role of a leader includes serving those like you who are in transition!

You may be the well for other people, yet you may not know how your work as an emerging leader will help others. You can trust that your connection and intervention may offer exactly the lift that another person touched by the storm needs!

Connections help you understand your transformation. Often the best mirror we have is other people; how we respond, what we can offer, how our emotions interpret circumstance. People can show you that you have moved out of the neutral zone, and help you understand the power of your gifts. Coming out of the storm, you may not be ready to see how you have grown, Your new connections will show you the potential greatness that you have prepared within you.

Cleanse your perceptions by removing old judgments about yourself. You have been through a crucible that brings out new strength of character. Don't depend on what you think you are capable of. You have new limits!

Learn about the expansion in your spirit by helping others. Leaders' talents are revealed in their work with other people. Leaders serve by lifting their colleagues to new levels of performance, acknowledging their dreams, and helping the community of followers succeed together. Great leaders don't just solve problems for others; they help to create new leaders. A transmission of spirit and kindness follows the engagement of a leader with an involved and ready follower.

Be willing to inspire and be inspired after the storm. You can build your network after the period of powerful storm energies. Some of your new connections will help you reach your goals. Others will teach you and mentor you. The outer circles of your trust radius can include many who never reveal how they have been changed by your work; you cannot know how your actions will influence others not engaged with your purpose. Accordingly, emerging leaders should hold optimism and conviction that they have brought goodness to their world, even if they do not see the fruits of their work directly.

RELATIONSHIPS SUPPORT YOUR GROWTH

Your relationships are a foundation to profound personal transformation. The people we know and touch make us stronger! Career-changers have told me how important other people are to them in supporting the new life they have imagined. "Success in any field, but especially in business, is about working with people, not against them," said Keith Ferrazzi (2004) in Never Eat Alone and other Secrets to Success. The relationships you have are partially under your control. If you are not surrounded by dynamic people, you are missing a chance to accelerate your growth.

> When we try to pick anything out by itself, we find it hitched to everything else in the universe.
> - John Muir

Your colleagues support you with what they know. If you are facing a challenge, your friends can provide their experience and wisdom to help you. Stay connected to your inner circle, and collaborate! A circle of friends acting as a mastermind group is a success strategy to help you face the barriers in your way. As you change your career and move through your neutral zone, the wisdom of your success-oriented relationships can lift you beyond the place of doubt.

Relationships can encourage the career-changer, and provide moral support. If I respect another person, and that person believes in me, well, WOW! I can go a bit further even if conditions are doubtful. My friends can lift my spirit, and it often starts with a willingness to listen and hold me in a respectful state. I can tell by the tone of the discussion if I receive respect, and it helps to make me resilient.

Your friends look after you. Their friends, and friends of friends, may be charged to help you fill a need. Good things can happen when a small community of people knows about a career-changer's purpose.

You've heard the idea of "six degrees of separation." Within our expanded circle of friends, colleagues and acquaintances are remarkable resources. Your key relationships won't let you down, so let them know what you are working on. Don't just present with requests ("I need to borrow a truck this week"); share what you are working on. Your community of close friends represents an incredible talent pool that can help you, if you permit them. Let others help you solve problems with their original thinking. They may be able to bring you closer to your career goals in ways that you had not even imagined!

The incredible power of your expanded network is that you do not have to possess great wisdom and experience in order to use it. If you have talented and experienced friends who believe in you, they will add their mental power to help you reach goals. Approach your friends with humility and confidence. Ask for the support that your friends might provide, and share your purpose. Your mental powers may suddenly expand through the supportive addition of your friends' efforts.

Do you want your relationship circle to be even more powerful? Then consciously approach your friends in the spirit of humble service that you might need of them. Be the kind of friend who can offer extraordinary support – perhaps not all the time, but when needed. Earn the right to use your relationships for assistance. Don't just be a "giver;" instead, look for ways that you can make your friends successful, too. Make this attitude of service a grateful manner that reflects all the opportunities you have been given to create your new career.

The well offers many possibilities to the traveler. To a person in transition, the well is a source of knowledge, and a connection to a community of achievers and people who believe in possibilities. When one drinks from the well regularly, many new perspectives and alternatives are open. The well offers a person in transition help from those nearby. After drinking from the well, a career-changer has more connections that help one reach goals, open markets, and influence others.

Drinking from the well helps to prevent fear. As a consequence of drinking from the well, new possibilities are seen which, in turn, dispel doubts about one's capacity to respond. The person in transition hastens to reach goals after being restored by the well.

How do you find your well? One must have an open mind, ready to accept new types of ideas. The discovery of the well is partly an act of grace, a favorable experience provided by a higher power. Regardless, I think the mind must be thirsting for help, and willing to take assistance from a foreign source.

CONNECTING WITH PEOPLE

Leaders build communities. The community may be a neighborhood, a nation, or a twibe (that's a tribe of like-minded people on Twitter). By proposing an organizing idea, leaders attract others with like-minded interest.

The career-changing leaders in my interviews vigorously offered the idea that connecting with other people was important in their journeys to become leaders. Emerging leaders cultivate a vision. Followers receive that vision, and place themselves into the picture.

If the career-changer has an idea of great potential, that idea may serve as the kernel for transformation. Powerful ideas change individuals. Once infected with a vision of great potential, people tend to share it with others. In this way, the career-changer may unintentionally "stumble" into the leader's role. The combination of a transformational idea expressed as a vision and the act of connecting with others regularly may be enough to establish a person as an emerging leader.

Once enough followers accept the leader's idea and vision, a community starts to coalesce. The career-changer may not have intended to build a community; nevertheless, a transformational idea can reorder social relationships. Leaders proceed on their life quest by serving the power of the vision.

Who is in charge–the leader, the vision, or the community? Great leaders follow the light of their vision. That light does not give them control of the vision. A vision tends to evolve, and leaders are not its only spokesperson. All members of a community may interpret and refine the vision.

FINDING YOUR WELL

To find your well, you must be connected to your center, and to the outer world. Both channels of inspiration, inner and outer, should be open on a regular basis. In addition, you will need two skills: Listening, and asking great questions. The person who connects to an internal source of knowing, to other people, and who practices the skills of listening and questioning will have access to an unquenchable source of knowledge and guidance.

Seek solitude. The internal world is frightening to some, yet it offers a stable platform of knowledge. Be willing to enter the silent, inner space with some reverence, respectful of the potential to gain the wisdom needed for all ventures. Create a home in your inner space. Make your connection with this center a constant in your life. Just as you need water every day, you will be nourished from your connection in the center.

Participate with the world of players, mentors, and colleagues. Lead with your heart, and support the people around you. Discover the issues that are important to the colleagues in your world. Ask, "How can I help?" whenever you hear someone in pain. You have a unique set of gifts to offer others. Show people how you contribute to a better world. Your connections can contribute to your well.

Bring two important skills to your inner life and connected circles. Approach your well with the right mindset of learning. An attitude of respectful inquiry can help you draw value from your well.

Cultivate the skill of listening. Bring your attention to the pulse of intelligence from your center. Calmly attend to the nature of the quiet source. I believe that the more the center is valued, the more value can come from the interior life. Listen and invest in this source of knowledge.

Be a good listener with others. There is a saying that we have been given two ears and one mouth, and we should listen and speak in that same two-to-one proportion. Listening opens the door to more insight.

Ask questions. Bring questions to your quiet center, and bring questions to the people in your world. Prepare your questions thoughtfully; let them be reconnaissance missions for intelligent information. If you lead people through change and into a better world, the questions you ask will help you lead your expedition through uncertainty. Plan your questions with the same determination that you would ask of any life transition.

After you have asked a question, release your concern with the answer. You have sent energy out to your well. You may not get the answer immediately. Be calm, and be grateful for the chance to hear the news that you need. Let the answer be prepared for you in its most useful form.

If you listen and question regularly, maintain a curious, receptive mind, and return to your center, you are likely to find your well. Its value to you will depend on how often you draw on the source of knowledge. If you value this well, then you may be blessed with regular insight to help you reach new goals.

SHARING YOUR WELL

You do not own your well of knowledge. You may contribute to it, draw from it regularly, and bring others to the same well. The well belongs to the community. If you have discovered lasting truth, this truth is not yours alone. The wisdom found in the well may be claimed by others, who will interpret it and present it with their unique gifts. If you work closely with your well, you have a trustee relationship with the knowledge at your disposal. Treat your well with high respect, and the well of knowledge may be yours to share with many.

When you share your well, you expand its value for all.

Sharing your well is more than pontificating or lecturing others. Many people do not respond appreciatively to direct gifts of knowledge. Instead, engage others with ideas, with the inspiration you have already received. Trust that others connect with the same source that you have been using. Try these techniques to help others share your well:

Use questions. Challenge the thinking of other people through a well-posed question. Questions practically force another person to consider the possibilities. When answering a question, a person's mind works to make a choice. Nothing wrong with a little mental workout, and the well opens up for a thirsty mind looking for answers!

Encourage others to see the possibilities. Hand a person a book, or tell that person that you noticed he or she thinks uniquely. Through encouragement, you help another person resonate with you. Appreciation opens the door to reluctant spirit. Show people that you have a depth of character in reserve. A good discussion may introduce another person to your well.

Practice collaboration. You don't have to be the most brilliant person in town. Ask for help in solving problems. Find a unique approach, and ask your colleague to suggest approaches. Think together, and let your well influence both of you. Collaboration forces a change in all partners. Through the joy of collaborative thinking and action, dissimilar spirits are brought into harmonious action.

THE LIGHT OF THE VISION

A leader's vision operates in the community. Like a beacon, a vision creates the light that illuminates the world of the possible. Many are attracted by a coherent vision. Light attracts people of who think about the world of the possible. Vision offers an appeal to the mind; it shows us what can be made of our efforts. As the leader speaks, promotes, and lives the vision, others are drawn into its luminescence. The leader helps to create community through use of a clear vision.

Consider, please, who owns the vision. If the leader generated the vision, is it his? I would place the ownership of the vision with the community assembled around the vision, but perhaps a vision is not "owned." It may have an intellectual value shared by all who hold it.

After all, does the owner of a flashlight own the light? Certainly, the bearer of a bright torch can direct the beam, yet all who enter the illumination may equally enjoy the light. The same could be said of a transformational vision. The leader can present the vision, decide where it will be shared, and add a certain presence and authentic depth of understanding to the vision.

Once the leader decides how the vision is presented, others start to share the vision as their own. The vision works like a meme, a carrier of information in a compact form. When a vision is presented well, it attracts the interest of others. Followers may grasp the concept, adapt the vision, and tweak the presentation in a new way. The light still spreads as a familiar variation.

Visions tend to evolve. Leaders are not the only spokespersons of a vision. The more people who grasp the essential idea, the more potent the force in the light can become. The power of the vision rightly belong to the tribe that shares its essence. The leader is like a grandfather to a transformational force that continues to live on beyond the leader's articulation of it.

CLOSING THOUGHT

The world can be a confusing place. Just when we think we know how the "game of life" works, the rules seem to change. A person with conviction and a vision can offer comfort and leadership to others going through the storm. Are you up to the challenge of leading others?

The person in career transition affects many others. When a positive decision to change work is made, other people will be consulted. Some will be touched by the uncertainty. Others may be lifted by the emotional decision to create something new. The career changer works in connection to others.

The storm of change is felt in the inner world, and the stormy weather extends through a network of relationships. We all go through the storm from time to time. This phase of life is inevitable for making new choices, determining a new direction. One choice is to become a leader and help other people through their period of the storm.

When you look for it, you may find the well of life wisdom. You may even contribute to it. Remember that you do not own this well, but you can help others drink from its nourishment. Let this elixir of knowledge help you make your most important choices.

Crystallize your vision. Keep talking about what is important. You have the chance to lift others, create other leaders, and help others find their way through the storm. The journey into leadership is more than a fulfillment of self-interest. Your work could increase happiness and enrich the work of others. Along the way, I believe your needs will be satisfied as well.

References

Adams, M. in Boshyk, Y. & Dilsworth, R.B. (2010). Action Learning and its Applications, Present and Future. St. Martin's Press, New York, NY.

Bennis, W. (1989). *On Becoming a Leader*, New York: Addison-Wesley Publishing Company.

Bennis, W. & Nanus, B. (2003). *Leaders*, New York: HarperBusiness.

Ferazzi, F. (2005). *Never Eat Alone and Other Secrets of Success.* New York: Crown Business.

Handy, C. (1996) *Beyond certainty.* Boston: Harvard Business School Press.

Kouzes, J. & Posner, B. (2002). *The leadership challenge.* San Francisco, CA: Jossey-Bass.

Maxwell, J. (2006). *The 360 degree Leader.* Nashville TN: Thomas Nelson Inc.

Sapolsky, R. (2004). *Why Zebras Don't Get Ulcers.* New York, NY. Henry Holt and Company, LLC, Holt Paperbacks.

Rath, T. (2007). *Strengthfinders 2.0.* New York: Gallup Press.

Townsend, R. (2007). *Up the Organization.* San Francisco, CA: Jossey-Bass.

www.ingramcontent.com/pod-product-compliance
Lightning Source LLC
Chambersburg PA
CBHW030940180526
45163CB00002B/646